A P[...] [STUDY]
OF WOMEN DEANS IN
COLLEGES AND UNIVERSITIES

By
JANE LOUISE JONES, Ph.D.

TEACHERS COLLEGE, COLUMBIA UNIVERSITY
CONTRIBUTIONS TO EDUCATION, No. 326

BUREAU OF PUBLICATIONS
Teachers College, Columbia University
NEW YORK CITY
1928

ACKNOWLEDGMENTS

I wish to express my sincere thanks to all those persons who have assisted me with this study. Of the faculty at Teachers College, Columbia University, I am greatly indebted to Dr. Harry D. Kitson for the impetus to apply modern methods of research to the unexplored field of the work of the dean and for much sagacious counsel and kindly encouragement; to Professor Sarah M. Sturtevant for the opportunity to specialize in her department and the inspiration of her teaching; and to Dr. Robert J. Leonard and Dr. Willystine Goodsell for many valuable suggestions with reference to the manuscript.

For time studies of their work, I owe thanks to Miss Eloise Pierce, Dean of Women, New York State College for Teachers, Albany, and to my sister, Miss Lydia I. Jones, Dean of Women, State Normal College, Ypsilanti, Michigan.

I have also to thank most cordially all the deans in colleges and universities who personally or by correspondence gave the information which made this investigation possible.

J. L. J.

CONTENTS

A PERSONNEL STUDY
OF WOMEN DEANS IN
COLLEGES AND UNIVERSITIES

CHAPTER I

THE PROBLEM

The history of the woman dean in college and university in this country begins, it appears, in the last decade of the nineteenth century, when outstanding pioneers in the field began their work. At the University of Chicago, Miss Marion Talbot was dean of women from 1892 to 1925. At the University of Michigan, Eliza Mosher, M.D., was dean of women from 1896 to 1909. At Northwestern University, Miss Mary Ross Potter was dean of women from 1903 until 1925. At Vassar College, Miss Ella McCaleb served as academic dean from 1913 to 1923, though for some years prior to 1913 she was performing the duties without the title.

During the twentieth century, because of the increase in the number of students in colleges and universities, the shift in the responsibility for students from the home to the college, and the present-day emphasis upon personnel work, there has come a steady increase in the number of deans for women students and the importance of their function in the public eye. New deanships have been established in many colleges and universities; since 1919 twenty-four courses have been organized in different institutions for the purpose of training deans; and the membership of the National Association of Deans of Women has increased from 18 in 1903 to 1,015 in 1927.[1]

Attendant upon this increase in the number of deans and in their importance has come considerable confusion of thought regarding the work which they should perform and the qualifications they should possess. Scattered attempts have been made to specify the types of work which deans should do, the qualifications they should have, how much they should be paid, and what academic privileges they should enjoy; but hitherto all such state-

[1] *Thirteenth Yearbook, National Association of Deans of Women, 1926.*

1

ments have been made without a complete study of existing conditions.

Indeed, the differences of opinion and practice in regard to the dean in various institutions have been so great that research workers have veered off from the field, despairing of ever obtaining any homogeneity of data. The need, however, for definite information about this vocation has grown apace and educators have begun to urge a modern scientific attack on the problem.

In the effort to learn something of conditions in this field, the writer has attempted this survey of deans of women in colleges, which may be used as a point of departure for future investigations. Two aims marked this investigation: (1) to discover certain facts about the women performing the function of dean in colleges and universities and to analyze their work; (2) on the basis of these facts, to make suggestions for the vocational guidance of deans and for the establishment of professional courses for deans.

The attempt was made to obtain objective data which might be used in answer to questions such as these:

1. How many women are now performing the function of dean in colleges in this country?
2. What titles do they hold?
3. What has been their academic training?
4. Do they teach?
5. If so, what subjects?
6. From what experience do they come into the work of a dean?
7. How long have they been in their present positions?
8. What salary do they receive?

For such a consideration of the characteristics of personality, such as sincerity, poise, and tact, which all will agree have much to do with the success or failure of a dean, we must wait for modern psychology to produce more satisfactory methods of measurement than it has yet evolved.

The analysis of the duties performed by deans will help us to answer the following questions:

1. With what duties are women deans chiefly engaged?
2. How, in view of the duties performed, can we classify deans?

Having gathered as much information as possible in answer to these questions, the writer endeavors to interpret it for the benefit of those who look to a college deanship as a vocational goal and for those who are giving and receiving professional training for the work.

To future investigators will remain the task of relating the work of deans to the various philosophies of education now taught in our colleges, of devising scientific methods for the selection of deans, and of developing special techniques to be used by the dean.

CHAPTER II

METHODS USED IN THE INVESTIGATION

The first requisite for an understanding of the work of dean, we have said in Chapter I, is an analysis of the occupation. To make such an analysis several techniques have been employed: the questionnaire, the interview, and the time study. For purposes of this investigation the probable advantages and disadvantages of each may be summarized.

The Questionnaire

The questionnaire has the advantage of being the most easily applied tool for an extensive survey. It is also, according to some investigators, likely to bring more accurate responses than the interview inasmuch as people tend to be more accurate in what they write than in what they say.

On the other hand, a questionnaire which is of value takes more time than busy people are usually able to give. To interpret the data about the dean's work in a given institution and draw reliable conclusions, one should have certain facts concerning the institution, organization, and equipment of the institution. If, for instance, a dean should answer that she does not supervise the extra-curricular activities, it would be important to know whether there were few extra-curricular activities on that campus, as might be the case in a municipal university attended chiefly by people who earn their living by day and study by night, or whether some other person in the institution had charge of the activities. To secure all the light on the situation would require a questionnaire of impossible dimensions.

A second objection is that deans who may have time to answer a questionnaire of reasonable length may not have the desire. Many are not yet interested in the scientific approach to their work. Some of those who are interested and would gladly co-operate in some plans are unsympathetic with personnel research and especially with the questionnaire.

4

A third objection to the questionnaire is that there are sure to be some questions that do not bring the desired information. In such cases the investigator can not, as in the interview, supplement or correct an inadequate reply by means of another question. Furthermore, persons may disregard questions which require considerable thought or seem too personal.

THE INTERVIEW

The interview is a more flexible tool and permits of a more intensive investigation. The interviewer can make all questions clear, can depart, if it seems wise, from the original plan, and by encouraging the person interviewed to volunteer information, can get many valuable suggestions for the future. In the investigation of a vocation with so many variables as that of dean, this method has distinct advantages.

It is evident, however, that because of the expenditure of time and money necessary for interviews, an investigation conducted by this method must resolve itself into case studies of the work of a very few persons, who may or may not be representative of the large body of deans. Moreover, one can not be certain of obtaining the necessary information by means of interviews. A dean, feeling that the exigency of the moment should supersede the demands of research, may be obliged to cancel her appointment for an interview after the interviewer has reached the campus. She may have interruptions while giving the interview. Or she may insist upon rambling. The information gathered may or may not be adequate. Again, its accuracy may be questionable. For example, a dean can not be expected to have at her tongue's end the number of students living in sorority houses in the college in which she serves. In an interview she can usually give only the approximate number.

THE TIME STUDY

A third method, known in the realm of industry as "time and motion study," seems to be the most scientific instrument yet devised for the analysis of a vocation. Popularized by Frederick W. Taylor and others in the early part of the twentieth century, this method has been used to great advantage in the analysis of trades.[1] It has distinguishing features:

[1] Taylor, Frederick. *The Principles of Scientific Management*, pp. 115-119.

a. The observation of the worker at his work by another person.

b. The breaking up of the work into minute components.

c. The measurement of the movements employed and the time spent for each component.

d. The accurate record kept by the observer.

This method seems superior to the questionnaire and the interview in that it is objective rather than subjective and permits of quantitative and exact measurement. Its exclusive use has not seemed advisable throughout this investigation, however, chiefly because of the variability of the work of deans in different institutions. A time study covering the work of one dean could not be used as the basis for vocational guidance or as important help in planning a curriculum for the training of deans unless we discovered that the work of deans in a number of institutions is similar. A time study might show one dean chiefly concerned with problems of health, the reason being that her institution, unlike the majority, had no health committee, resident physician, or infirmary. It might show that in one college the dean teaches thirty-two hours a week, but it would not show that this was the only one of two hundred and sixty-three institutions where the dean had so heavy a teaching schedule.

Moreover, the work not only varies from one institution to another, but it varies in a given institution according to the time of year. In the autumn, a dean may be chiefly concerned with housing; directly after the mid-year examinations she may spend the greatest part of her time in interviews; during Junior Week her days and nights are likely to be filled with social responsibilities. For full information concerning the duties of a single dean, a time study would have to record her activities for at least a year. Indeed, some deans would say for several years, inasmuch as they have for a year at a time devoted all their energies to one task, such as raising money or equipping a dormitory.

Another objection that might be raised to the use of this method of analyzing the work of a dean is that it might interfere with the dean's daily work. Let us say the entire morning is spent in interviews with students. Much of the conversation that takes place will be so personal that the dean would not be justified in having the person who is to keep the record invisible, listening to the student who is unconscious of a third person. If the observer is visible, her presence is likely to prove a deterrent to free expression on the part of the person interviewed, if not of the interviewer. No one apparently has ever suggested that a dean might dispense with the observer and keep her own record, nor has anyone studied the relative proportion of interviews that are confidential in nature and those that are impersonal.

Inasmuch as each of these three methods appears to have distinct advantages and no one of them seems sufficient in itself, the investigator decided to employ all three in the hope that the assembled data would give some facts about all women deans in colleges, detailed information about the work of a certain group, and an accurate quantitative study of the work of a sample group for a short period of time.

The steps in the investigation were as follows:

1. *Questionnaire Sent to Presidents of Institutions.*[2] It was necessary first to ascertain which colleges have a woman member of the faculty representing the interests of women students, her exact title in each, and her name. Since no published list proved complete or accurate, a letter was sent by the writer, November, 1925, to the president of each college attended by women which was listed in the Educational Directory, Department of the Interior, 1925. The questionnaire, multigraphed on the official stationery of Teachers College, was signed by Professors Sarah M. Sturtevant and H. D. Kitson, who were sponsoring the investigation. Only three items of information were asked for: whether the institution had a woman performing the function of dean, her title, and her name. A stamped addressed envelope was enclosed, and it was necessary for the president or his secretary to make only two check marks, write the name of the dean, sign his own, fold the sheet, slip it into the envelope, and seal.

2. *Questionnaire Addressed to Registrars of Institutions.* The returns from this questionnaire showed that whereas a large percentage of institutions have a woman dean, some excellent colleges do not. From occasional comments written by the presidents on the questionnaires, it seemed likely that the enrollment of women in the college might be the determining factor. Accordingly, a request was sent to the registrar of each institution, asking for the number of men students and the number of women enrolled in the spring session of 1926, excluding those in extension and extra-mural courses.

[2] See Appendix, page 144, for Questionnaire I.

3. *Interviews*. From the list of women deans whose names were reported in the answers to Questionnaire I, twenty-four were selected to be interviewed for the purpose of discovering the vocational history of each and the most important of her duties. The sampling included deans from colleges of various types, in various parts of the country, and of varying sizes,—coeducational, independent colleges for women, affiliated colleges for women, colleges publicly supported and privately endowed, nonsectarian, and denominational colleges. The only characteristics common to all the institutions represented in the list were: the presence of women students, a woman officially appointed to supervise them, and inclusion in the list of institutions accredited by the Association of American Universities. The last item was made a determining factor in the selection because it seemed likely that these institutions which have achieved the highest standards in entrance requirements, courses of study, qualifications of the faculty, and equipment would present the function of the dean in its most highly developed form.

Guided by experience gained as assistant in courses of instruction for advisers of women in Teachers College, the investigator drew up a list of questions and submitted it to several deans of women and revised it in accordance with the suggestions received. It was then used as a basis for interviews with the twenty-four deans. Five were interviewed in their own offices, three in New York City, and sixteen at the annual meeting of the National Association of Deans of Women held in Washington, February, 1926.

The duration of the interviews ranged from one-half of an hour to two hours. For each, a mimeographed copy of standardized questions was used on which answers were recorded. In general, the answers were clear-cut and full, and the deans were very generous in making suggestions to further the investigation.

4. *Vocational History Sheet Sent to All Women Deans*. In the use of this sheet, the writer followed the method of Kitson,[3] who has recently demonstrated how the vocational history may be used as an instrument for vocational guidance.

The sheet was sent to the 394 deans whose names were sub-

[3] Kitson, Harry D. "A Preliminary Personnel Study of Psychologists." *Psychological Review*, Vol. 33, No. 4, July, 1926.

Kitson, Harry D. "The Scientific Compilation of Vocational Histories as a Method to be Used in Vocational Guidance," *Teachers College Record*, September, 1926.

mitted by the presidents of colleges. The information asked for was concerned with degrees, teaching, academic rank, experience, and salary. The exact title was also requested and the reply was compared with that given previously by the president to the same question in answer to Questionnaire I. For the deans of Group I, the items were made a part of the long questionnaire sent to this group, and other matters were added, such as family status, church affiliation, academic honors, foreign travel, and professional courses taken. Consequently, on some points discussed in later chapters, returns are cited for only 107 deans in Group I, and on others they are given for all the 263 deans in the three groups who sent replies.

For this sheet any question was omitted if it had not previously brought significant data in personal interviews with deans. The matter of secondary school training, for instance, was dropped since the findings showed no preponderance of persons from either private or public secondary schools. Other questions were omitted because they might tend to diminish the number of replies. It was decided, for example, not to ask for age or total number of years of experience, although such data would have had great significance. It was considered very important to confine this questionnaire to a single page on the theory that the shorter the questionnaire, the greater the number of returns.

5. *Questionnaire Sent to Women Performing the Function of Dean in Institutions Approved by the Association of American Universities.*[4] Since it was evident that a long, detailed questionnaire of eight pages could not be sent to the deans of all colleges, it was decided to send it only to deans in colleges approved by the Association of American Universities. With the results of the interview as a guide, the investigator drew up a set of questions which aimed to evoke definite and rather detailed information concerning the duties of the dean. Although this was long and reached the deans at Commencement time when they were particularly busy, it elicited response from seventy per cent of them. Since the questions differed in certain particulars from those asked of the twenty-four deans previously interviewed, the questionnaire was sent to those deans with the request that they supply the additional information. Twenty complied with the request.

6. *Time Study of the Work of Two Deans.* In addition to the

[4] See Questionnaire IV, page 147.

exhaustive investigation described above, the investigator conducted still more minute studies covering the work of two deans for two weeks. The purpose was to find out what duties the dean performed in a given period and the time spent on each. A standardized plan was used for classifying the duties and keeping the record. One dean kept her own; the other requested her secretary to observe and record everything that the dean did on behalf of the institution. A detailed account of the technique is found in Chapter XI.

CHAPTER III

NUMBER OF WOMEN PERFORMING THE FUNCTION OF DEAN

To all persons concerned with the higher education of women, it is interesting to know in how many institutions in this country women are employed as deans and in which institutions they serve. To ascertain this information, Questionnaire I was sent to the presidents of all colleges accredited and nonaccredited which were attended by women.[1] Of this list of five hundred and three, one hundred fifty-eight are approved by the Association of American Universities. These institutions are referred to as Group I in this report. One hundred twenty-nine are approved by some one of the following standardizing agencies: the Association of Colleges and Secondary Schools of the Southern States, the North Central Association of Colleges and Secondary Schools, and the Northwest Association of Secondary and Higher Schools. In this report these one hundred twenty-nine constituted Group II. The remaining two hundred sixteen, not accredited by any of the agencies mentioned, make up Group III. It should be noted that the last four agencies mentioned above include all colleges in the United States except those in New England and the far West; hence if a college in either of these sections is not approved by the Association of American Universities, which is national in scope, it is perforce classed in this report with Group III. Teachers colleges are not included in the investigation unless included in the list of the Association of American Universities.[2]

The returns from this questionnaire are shown in Table I, where it can be seen that the number of replies received from Group I was 158, or 100 per cent of the number sent. From Group II, there were 124, or 96 per cent, making a total for accredited colleges of 282, or 98.2 per cent. These unusually good returns

[1] See page 144 of Appendix.
[2] *Accredited Higher Universities*, American Council on Education, Washington, D. C.

may be accounted for by the facts that presidents of higher institutions of this grade have grown increasingly conscious of the need for definite information in this field and that the questionnaire was easy to answer. The number received from Group III was 140, or 64 per cent. Possible reasons for a poorer showing from this group are: less interest in this sort of research, less secretarial help in the offices of the presidents, and the feeling that the reply would not be of value if the institution had no dean. Furthermore, to the few accredited colleges which did not reply promptly, a second request was sent. This was not done in the case of the nonaccredited colleges.

The first question read, "Does your institution have a woman officially appointed to supervise the college life among women students; as academic programs, housing, social activities, vocational guidance?" The nature of the appointment was emphasized because in some institutions without a dean, a member of the faculty not officially appointed to the duties assumes them. In such cases, it was thought the presidents might send in the names of those persons. The point was not whether the interests of

TABLE I

COLLEGES AND UNIVERSITIES HAVING WOMAN DEAN

INSTITUTIONS BY ACADEMIC RATING	NUMBER OF INSTITUTIONS	NUMBER REPLYING	PER CENT REPLYING	NUMBER HAVING DEAN	PER CENT OF THOSE REPLYING HAVING DEAN
Group I	158	158	100	154	97.4
Group II	129	124	96.1	117	94.3
Group III	216	140	64.1	123	87.8
Total	503	422	83.9	394	93.3

women are looked after (presumably they are in any institution which admits women), but whether there was one woman officially appointed to the task. The second question asked for her title, and the third for her name.

In general, the replies were clear cut. A few institutions, such as Yale and Harvard, which admit women only to certain graduate schools, replied that theirs are colleges for men. To these it was necessary to send a second communication asking if there was an adviser or dean of women for graduate students. Many presidents, particularly in colleges for women, wrote letters to accompany the questionnaires, explaining that whereas academic problems were taken care of by a dean, the housing, social activities, and vocational guidance were taken care of by other members of the faculty appointed for such work. It was found that in four cases the president of a college misunderstood the question and sent in as the name of the dean that of a person who later disclaimed the title, saying she merely helped out with the girls because there was no dean. In two cases the person received no salary from the college for any services; in one she was the wife of the president and in the other a wealthy patroness of the institution who gave certain services in addition to money. These four institutions were not counted as having officially appointed deans.

It was decided in all other cases to include in the list and to use as the subjects of further investigation:

1. The person who in the mind of the president obviously fitted the description, whatever her title might be.
2. The dean, in case the president mentioned both a dean and an associate dean.
3. The dean, in case the president stated that the interests of women students were looked after by an academic dean and by other persons such as vocational director, social director, or student counsellor.
4. The academic dean, in case the president mentioned both academic dean and "dean of residence." If the only person mentioned was the dean of residence, she was included.

The deans of liberal arts colleges such as Barnard, which is a college for women forming a part of Columbia University, are included. The deans of separate professional schools such as a School of Home Economics are not included, with the exception of one who is dean of the College of Home Economics and dean of women for an entire institution.

NUMBER OF DEANS

Of the institutions in Group I, 154, or 97 per cent of those approved by the Association of American Universities, replied that they had a woman officially appointed to supervise the various phases of the college life of women students. In Group II, 117, or 94 per cent of those replying, claimed a dean, the total number of accredited colleges being 271, or 96 per cent. In Group III, 123, which is 88 per cent of those replying, answered affirmatively. The total in all colleges is 394, or 93 per cent, of the 422 institutions replying.

It is interesting to note the type of institution in these various groups which replied in the negative. In Group I there are four: Clark University, Worcester, Mass., has only fifty-three women students, all of whom are graduates. Massachusetts Institute of Technology, Cambridge, Mass., has highly specialized courses with forty-five women students. The College of St. Elizabeth, Convent Station, New Jersey, is a Roman Catholic institution with 182 women. Johns Hopkins is credited with 1,878 women. In the first two institutions the number of women students obviously does not justify a woman dean. At the College of St. Elizabeth the absence of a dean is undoubtedly due to its organization by which there is a division of the duties ordinarily performed by a dean among various members of the faculty who keep in close touch with the students. At Johns Hopkins, the lack of a woman dean is less easily explained.

In Group II, the institutions replying that they have no dean are: Creighton University, Omaha, Neb., which explains that the women are in a separate college with the Religious of the Sacred Heart in charge; Gettysburg College, Gettysburg, Pa., which states that it has only seventy-five women students, all of whom are day students; Hendrix College, Conway, Arkansas, with only sixty-five women; Jamestown College, Jamestown, N. D., which has for its one hundred eighty women a system of faculty sponsors and a matron of the dormitory; University of Hawaii, University of Louisville, and Upper Iowa University, which gave no explanation.

In the seventeen colleges in Group III which have no dean, the absence is probably explained by the small enrollment which permits individual teachers to perform the duties under supervision of the president.

We can, therefore, conclude that there are, at least, 394 women in the colleges of the country who serve as dean, though, as will be shown later, under varying conditions.

Title. The reply to the second query of the questionnaire

showed that among the 394 institutions represented, seventeen different titles were held by the women performing the function of dean. These titles, with the frequency of their occurrence, are as follows:

TITLE	FREQUENCY
Adviser	15
Chairman of Activities Committee	1
Chairman of Student Affairs Committee	1
Chairman of Women's University Council	1
Counsellor	7
Dean	26
Dean of Residence	1
Dean of Students	3
Dean of Women	322
Hostess	2
Matron	1
Preceptress	2
Regent	1
Representative of Women	1
Social Directress	2
Supervisor of Women	1
Warden	1
Title omitted	6
Total	394

It is noteworthy that in 82 per cent of the institutions studied, the person appointed has the title of dean of women. The only other titles which occur with a frequency that is significant are dean (which means dean of the college) and adviser, the first occurring in seven per cent of the cases and the second in four per cent.

In general, these titles connote something of the duties performed by the person holding them. The title of dean, or dean of the college, further investigation showed, usually goes with a preponderance of academic duties. A social director is sure to have as her first interest the social life of the college. A counsellor spends most of her time in personnel work; an adviser advises. The title which is least descriptive of all is dean of women. The person thus designated may have a place recognized and powerful in shaping the academic policies in one of our greatest universities, or she may be concerned with the smallest details of the housekeeping in a dormitory. She may spend the largest portion of her time in personnel work in her office, and she has been known to make more than two hundred off-campus speeches in a year. There are, however, certain duties which it appears are performed by a large percentage of deans of women and a considerable percentage of all deans; and these are the ones which this investigation was planned to disclose.

The popularity of the title, dean of women, has undoubtedly been strengthened by the regulation made by the American Association of University Women that, to be on its approved list, a college should have a woman dean or dean of women.[3] In some instances, the title has been given under protest, though the person carrying it had practically no academic duties. In a few cases the title has been given accompanied by considerable academic power. In others, the institution has used some other title.

Our examination of the 422 responses to Questionnaire I, therefore, shows that 394, or 93 per cent, of the colleges and universities replying have a woman officially appointed to serve as dean. The higher the academic rank of the college, the more likely it is to have a dean. In 322, or 82 per cent, of the cases she bears the title of dean of women. In 26, or 7 per cent, she is called dean, or dean of the college. In 15, or 4 per cent, she has the title of adviser.

[3] *Information on Membership for Colleges and Universities.* American Association of University Women, 1925.

CHAPTER IV

EDUCATIONAL HISTORIES OF DEANS

The Vocational History Sheet described in Chapter II was sent to the dean of each of the 394 institutions which had replied that it had a woman dean. Of these, 263, or 66.7 per cent, returned the questionnaire. Table II shows the proportion of institutions in each group which returned the sheet.

TABLE II

VOCATIONAL HISTORY

ITEM	CLASSIFICATION OF INSTITUTION								TOTAL OF ALL COLLEGES	
	Group I		Group II		Total I and II		Group III			
	No.	Per Cent	No.	Per Cent	No.	Per Cent	No.	Per Cent	No.	Per Cent
Questionnaires sent ..	154	......	117	......	271	....	123	......	394	......
Replies	107	69.7	82	70.0	189	69.7	74	60.1	263	66.7

See Questionnaire II, page 145.

The three types of educational experience considered on the sheet were academic training, a professional course for deans, and foreign travel. Concerning academic training, for which degrees which are held by deans have been taken as a measure, the investigation included the 263 deans in all three groups; in regard to a professional course for deans and foreign travel it was concerned only with the 107 deans in Group I.

ACADEMIC DEGREES

Of the deans in Group I, 95 per cent have at least the Bachelor's degree. (See Table III.) The others, though they have not taken systematic work leading to a degree, are, the investigator discovered, women of considerable erudition. In Group II, 88 per cent have at least the Bachelor's degree; in Group III, 86 per cent. Altogether 238, or 91 per cent, of the deans in all groups hold at least the Bachelor's degree.

The Master's degree is held by 72, or 68 per cent, in Group I; by 46, or 56 per cent, in Group II; and by 33, or 44 per cent, in Group III. In all, the Master's degree is held by 151 deans, or 57 per cent, of the whole number. The explanation of this high frequency doubtless lies in the fact that 70 per cent of the deans teach, and as college teachers they feel the need of at least one year of graduate work which is usually required for the Master's degree.

TABLE III

Degrees Held by Women Deans

(263 Cases)

DEGREE	GROUP I							
	Coed.*		W.I.*		W.A.*		Total	
	No.	Per Cent	No.	Per Cent	No.	Per Cent	No.	Per Cent
No Degree	5	6.0	....	....	....	......	5	4.6
Bachelor's	79	94.0	17	100	6	100	102	95.3
Master's	58	69.0	10	58.0	4	66	72	67.9
Doctor's	14	16.6	12	70.5	3	50	29	27.0

DEGREE	GROUP II		GROUP III		TOTAL ALL GROUPS	
	No.	Per Cent	No.	Per Cent	No.	Per Cent
No Degree	10	12.1	10	13.5	25	9.5
Bachelor's	72	87.8	64	86.4	238	90.5
Master's	46	56.0	33	44.5	151	57.4
Doctor's	7	8.5	4	5.4	40	15.2

Coed. = Coeducational College
W.I. = Women's Independent College
W.A. = Women's Affiliated College

The Doctor's degree is held by 29, or 27 per cent, of Group I; by 7, or 9 per cent, of Group II; and by 4, or 5 per cent, of Group III—altogether by 15 per cent of all the deans studied. In the 17 independent colleges for women in Group I, in which, as we shall see in Chapter X, the dean is first of all an "academic" dean, 12, or 70 per cent, of the deans hold the Doctor's degree.

In order to ascertain whether the figure of 27 per cent for the number of deans with Doctor's degrees in Group I is relatively large or small, it should be compared with the number of Doctor's degrees held by women college teachers at large. In order to have some figures for comparison, a study was made

TABLE IV

NUMBER OF WOMEN ON FACULTY WITH DOCTOR'S DEGREES IN FIVE COLLEGES

COLLEGE	NUMBER OF WOMEN ON FACULTY	NUMBER WITH DOCTOR'S DEGREE	PER CENT WITH DOCTOR'S DEGREE
Bryn Mawr	32	16	50
Smith	132	41	31
Vassar	96	48	50
Wells	25	10	40
Wheaton	26	9	35
Total	311	124	40

among women members of faculties of five women's colleges in Group I: Bryn Mawr, Smith, Vassar, Wells, and Wheaton. Results are shown in Table IV, where it will be seen that forty per cent, in addition to the deans, hold the Doctor's degree—fifteen per cent more than the number of deans in Group I. A comprehensive study of the degrees held by women teachers in all the colleges in Group I would probably show that the proportion of the persons holding this degree is considerably larger than the percentage of deans who do. The work of a dean is varied, and calls for so many different qualifications that in the selection of a dean advanced academic training has frequently given way to characteristics, such as executive ability, a winning personality, and an understanding of youth.

ACADEMIC HONORS

An inquiry into the academic honors received by the deans in Group I shows that 76 honors are distributed among 54 persons, that is, 50 per cent of the entire number have received one of the honors listed in Table V. It should be explained, moreover, that some deans took their undergraduate training in institutions which at the time had no chapters of Phi Beta Kappa or Sigma Xi and that fellowships and scholarships have in recent years become more numerous. The data gathered are interesting but hardly indicative of the academic attainment of all deans.

TABLE V

ACADEMIC HONORS OF WOMEN DEANS IN GROUP I

(107 Cases)

HONORS	DISTRIBUTION OF HONORS							
	Coed. *		W.I.*		W.A.*		Total	
	No.	Per Cent	No.	Per Cent	No.	Per Cent	No.	Per Cent
Phi Beta Kappa	22	26.2	9	52.9	4	66.7	35	32.7
Sigma Xi	2	2.4					2	1.9
Fellowships	14	16.7	6	35.3	2	33.3	22	20.6
Scholarships	6	7.1	4	23.5	1	16.7	11	10.3
Honorary Degrees	5	6.0	1	5.9			6	5.6
Total Honors	49		20		7		76	
Persons with Honors	40	47.6	10	58.8	4	66.7	54	50.5
Persons with No Honors	44	52.4	7	41.2	2	33.3	53	49.5
Total	84		17		6		107	

Coed. = Coeducational College
W.I. = Women's Independent College
W.A. = Women's Affiliated College

PROFESSIONAL COURSE FOR DEANS

Of the deans in Group I, 21, or 20 per cent, have taken a professional course for deans. This is a small number. It may be accounted for on several grounds: first, the courses are still young—the earliest having been established in 1916 at Teachers College, Columbia University—and they are still in an experimental stage. Second, a number of the courses, since they emphasized the work of the high school more than that of the college dean have attracted more teachers from secondary schools than from colleges. Third, many deans having taken graduate work in their teaching subjects have not felt that they could afford to superimpose upon that study the professional course for deans. Fourth, others who sought study bearing directly upon the work of a dean have met their need by taking a group of subjects in the regular academic curriculum, such as philosophy, psychology, sociology, and hygiene, and have tried to apply the facts which they have learned to their work as dean. Fifth, some deans without professional training have met with marked success in their work and, in consequence, do not see the advantage of a professional course for themselves or for prospective deans. They maintain toward professional training for the work the same attitude that successful physicians had toward professional training for medicine when it was in its infancy and lawyers had toward the professionalized course in law.

In view of all these factors, it is encouraging to note that one-fifth of the deans in 107 of the colleges of highest academic rank have taken at least one professional course for deans, though the

TABLE VI

PROFESSIONAL COURSE TAKEN BY WOMEN IN GROUP I

(107 Cases)

ITEM	GROUP I						TOTAL	
	Coed.		W.I.		W.A.			
	No.	Per Cent	No.	Per Cent	No.	Per Cent	No.	Per Cent
Replies to Question ..	84	......	17	......	6	......	107	......
Number Having Taken Course	20	23.8	0	0	1	16.6	21	19.6

limited number gives evidence that the work of dean is still regarded by some persons as an adjunct of a professorship in
English, Latin, or some other subject, rather than as a distinct
profession in itself.

Foreign Travel

To-day more than ever, foreign travel is considered a desirable
means of education. It is encouraging to note that of the 107
deans in Group I, 61 per cent have had foreign travel involving, in many cases, several trips of an extended stay of months
or years.

Summary

Stated briefly, the facts concerning the education of women
deans in colleges and universities are these:

Of 263 deans comprising Groups I, II, and III, 238, or 90 per
cent, hold the Bachelor's degree. One hundred fifty-one, or 57
per cent, hold the Master's degree. The higher the academic
rank of the institution, the greater the percentage of deans holding each degree.

Concerning the 107 deans in Group I, it should be noted that
deans in colleges for women are more likely to hold the Doctor's
degree than are those in coeducational institutions. Fifty-four, or
50 per cent, of Group I have received the academic honor of membership in Phi Beta Kappa or Sigma Xi, a fellowship, a scholarship, or an honorary degree. Twenty-one, or 20 per cent, have
taken a professional course for deans. Sixty-five, or 61 per cent,
have travelled abroad.

CHAPTER V

ACADEMIC RANK OF DEANS

Women deans have relatively high academic rank. Of the total number, 197, or 75 per cent, have some academic rank, though only 71 per cent teach. There are 173, or 66 per cent, who hold rank above that of instructor. Of the deans in coeducational institutions in Group I, 67, or 80 per cent, have academic rank, though as we shall see in Chapter X, they have officially less to do with academic duties than do deans in women's colleges. The rank most commonly found is that of professor, which is held by 105, or 40 per cent, of all the 263 deans. In the colleges of Group I, 49 deans, or 46 per cent, are professors.

It is surprising to find concerning the deans of all groups that of those who are full professors only 28, or 29 per cent, hold the Doctor's degree, although it is often difficult for other members of a college faculty to attain to a professorship without that degree. Tables VII and VIII serve to show a comparison of the degrees held by deans who hold the rank of full professor in the colleges

TABLE VII

DEGREES OF DEANS IN GROUP I HAVING RANK OF FULL PROFESSOR

(107 Colleges)

DEGREE	FREQUENCY			TOTAL
	Coed.	W. I.	W. A.	
No Degree				
A.B.	9	1	1	11
A.M.	19		1	20
Ph.D. and M.D.	6	9	2	17
Total	34	10	4	48

TABLE VIII

DEGREES HELD BY WOMEN FULL PROFESSORS IN TWENTY COLLEGES
FOR WOMEN

COLLEGE	FREQUENCY				TOTAL
	No. Degree	B.S. or B.A. Only	M.S. or M.A. Only	Ph.D. or M.D.	
Barnard	—	—	—	1	1
Bryn Mawr	—	1	1	8	10
Connecticut College for Women	—	—	—	2	2
Goucher	—	—	—	12	12
Illinois Women's College	1	—	8	—	9
Florida State College	—	—	3	5	8
Lake Erie College	1	—	6	7	14
Mt. Holyoke	1	4	3	22	30
Randolph-Macon Women's College	1	—	—	2	3
Smith	2	—	4	13	19
Sophie Newcomb	2	—	3	1	6
Sweet Briar	—	—	3	5	8
University of Richmond	1	—	—	3	4
Vassar	1	—	1	22	24
Wells	1	—	2	6	9
Western Reserve	—	3	1	0	4
Wheaton College	—	—	4	0	4
William Smith	—	1	—	—	1
Wilson	2	1	6	7	16
Total	13	10	45	116	184
Per Cent	7	5	23	65	100

of Group I and the degrees of the women full professors in twenty
colleges selected from that group. Of the 48 deans in Group I
holding the rank of full professor, 17, or 35 per cent, hold the
Doctor's degree. Of the 185 women full professors in 20 colleges,
121, or 65 per cent, hold the degree.

Of the 263 deans considered in the present study, 54, that is,
51 per cent of the full professors, have no degree beyond the
Master's degree; 20, or 19 per cent, have only the Bachelor's degree

and 3 have no degree at all. As might be expected, the majority of deans who hold no degree have no academic rank whatever.

It is interesting to compare these figures with some presented in two previous studies of academic rank. In a study made by Committee N of the American Association of University Professors, it was reported that in the 104 universities and colleges noted, 26 per cent have no women of professional rank in the liberal arts departments, while 47 per cent have no women holding full professorship.[1]

A later study of the academic status of women on university faculties presented by Miss Lohn before the American Association of University Women states that, in 70 universities noted, only 28 women enjoyed the title of full professor in strictly academic subjects as compared with 21,000 men. Eighteen universities had women who are full professors, while 43 had none.[2]

The per cent of women professors would have been larger if Miss Lohn had included in her study professors of home economics, physical education, music, arts, agriculture, and education as well as technical lines. She limited herself strictly to teachers of the so-called liberal arts subjects, whereas the present writer is considering deans regardless of the subject they teach. Nevertheless, all the evidence seems to show that deans, in general, hold comparatively high academic rank.

In the course of the investigation the writer found three main reasons for this. The first lies in the fact that many deans have been teachers and have continued to teach after they became deans. Frequently they achieved their rank as teachers in the very institutions in which they are now serving as deans. Seventy per cent are still teaching.

The second reason is found in the reluctance of deans to give up academic rank when obliged, by the pressure of other duties, to relinquish their teaching. Deans appear to guard their rank jealously, once it is attained. It gives them, particularly if it was earned by academic achievements prior to appointment as dean, a certain academic prestige with their *confrères* and with the students on the campus. It frequently entails a place on certain academic committees and an opportunity to work for educational policies which they would not otherwise have. To have

[1] *Bulletin of the American Association of University Professors,* October, 1921.
[2] "Academic Status of Women on University Faculties." Reprint from the *Journal of American Association of University Women,* 1924.

TABLE IX

ACADEMIC RANK HELD BY WOMEN DEANS

(263 Cases)

RANK ON FACULTY	GROUP I						TOTAL	
	COED.		W. I.		W. A.			
	No.	Per Cent	No.	Per Cent	No.	Per Cent	No.	Per Cent
Lecturer	1	1.2	—	—	—	—	1	.9
Instructor	3	3.6	1	5.9	–	—	4	3.7
Assistant Professor	15	17.9	1	5.9	1	16.7	17	15.9
Associate Professor	13	15.5	2	11.8	1	16.7	16	15.0
Professor	35	41.7	10	58.8	4	66.6	49	45.8
Total with Rank	67	79.9	14	82.4	6	100.0	87	81.3
Without Rank	17	20.2	3	17.6	0	—	20	18.7
Total Deans ..	84	100.0	17	100.0	6	100.0	107	100.0

RANK ON FACULTY	GROUP II		GROUP III		TOTAL ALL GROUPS	
	No.	Per Cent	No.	Per Cent	No.	Per Cent
Lecturer	—	—	—	—	1	.4
Instructor	8	9.8	11	14.9	23	8.8
Assistant Professor	12	14.6	5	6.8	34	12.9
Associate Professor	8	9.8	10	13.5	34	12.9
Professor	30	36.6	26	35.1	105	39.9
Total with Rank	58	70.0	52	70.3	197	74.9
Without Rank	24	29.3	22	29.7	66	25.1
Total Deans	82	100.0	74	100.0	263	100.0

the rank of professor is an asset in case they wish to leave the vocation of dean and teach exclusively.

The third contributing factor to the large percentage of deans with academic rank is the type of college or university organization which necessitates making a dean a professor if she is to have a salary commensurate with the importance of the duties she performs. A dean of women, for example, in a state institution, holding the rank of assistant professor now receives the maximum salary paid to teachers of that rank. If her salary is to be increased, her rank must be advanced to that of associate professor. Such advancement may seem inappropriate and difficult if she is doing no teaching and can find time for none. The only satisfactory solution for such a problem, some institutions have found, is a change in the administration of the budget which

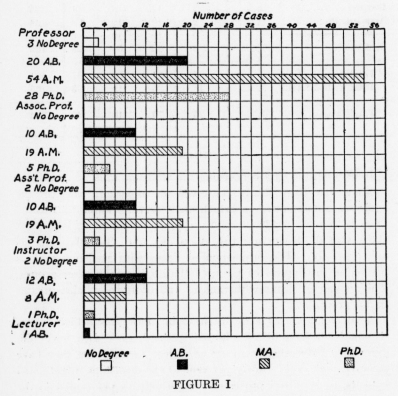

FIGURE I

DEGREE AND ACADEMIC RANK OF 263 DEANS

makes the dean of women an administrative officer with an appropriate salary and no academic rank. This change, though it deprives deans of academic prestige, appears to be a step in the evolution of the dean from a teacher to an administrative officer.

TABLE X

ACADEMIC RANK OF WOMEN DEANS AND DEGREES HELD

(263 Cases)

RANK	No DEGREE	DEGREE			TOTAL
		A.B. Only	A.B. and A.M. Only	Ph.D.	
Lecturer	—	1	—	—	1
Instructor	2	12	8	1	23
Assistant Professor	2	10	19	3	34
Associate Professor...........	0	10	19	5	34
Professor	3	20	54	28	105
Total with Rank	7	53	100	37	197
Total without Rank	18	26	19	3	66
Total Deans	25	79	119	40	263

SUMMARY

In general, the data concerning the academic rank of 263 deans indicate that these deans are given an important place in the academic communities in which they serve. Three-fourths of them hold some academic rank; 173, or 66 per cent, hold rank above that of instructor; 105, or 40 per cent, hold the rank of full professor. The proportion of deans with academic rank is greater in institutions of Group I than it is in the other groups. The number of deans with rank of full professor is also greater in this group.

A consideration of rank in the light of degrees held indicates that not only have deans achieved academic rank with fewer degrees than have other members of college faculties but they have achieved high rank. Forty per cent of the deanships investigated hold the rank of full professor though only 15 per cent hold the Doctor's degree.

CHAPTER VI

DEANS AS TEACHERS

Information that is of great importance to rational consideration of this vocation is the answer to the question, "Are deans teachers as well as deans?" It is a question raised by college presidents who, as they make a new appointment to a deanship, seek to follow the most approved plan of organization for the office. Upon the answer may depend other appointments to the teaching staff, the number of assistants assigned to the deans, her academic rank, her salary, and even the underlying conception of the office itself. It matters not what type of dean is contemplated, the decision as to whether or not the dean shall teach is one of significance in college administration.

The question is also raised by women who have as their vocational aim a college deanship in which social duties predominate. Are there deanships, they wish to know, open to social workers, leaders of the Girl Scouts, and administrative officers of the Young Women's Christian Association who have no experience in teaching or predilection for the work but do have experience and skill in dealing with young women? Academic deans in colleges for women, they know they can not be; deans of women in coeducational institutions, they would like to be.

Again, for the persons planning professional courses for deans the information concerning the percentage of deans who teach is of vital importance. Obviously, if most deans teach, they must take graduate work in their teaching subject and make a proper division of time between study for teaching and study for the duties of dean.

NUMBER OF DEANS WHO TEACH

Of the 263 college deans studied in this investigation, it was found that 187, or 72 per cent, were teaching in addition to performing the functions of dean. The academic standing of the college has apparently little bearing on the matter, for in Group

I the number is 70 per cent; in Group II, 71 per cent; and in Group III, 73 per cent. In Group I there is practically no difference between the per cent of deans teaching in the 84 coeducational institutions and the per cent of those teaching in the 16 independent colleges for women. Of the six colleges for women allied to other institutions, three deans teach and three do not.

In attempting to discover why some deans teach and some do not, the writer found that many in the larger institutions are teaching from choice although the heads of the institutions would be glad to relieve them of classroom work. The deans give as reasons: the pleasure they derive from teaching; the contact with students they can get in no other way; the academic prestige entailed and a seat in academic councils; and the advantage of keeping up-to-date in a teaching subject to which they may wish to return. Two of these reasons, it may be noted, are among those given for desiring academic rank. In a few institutions teaching means additional salary. In smaller colleges there is a tendency to expect the dean to teach, since the small enrollment is supposed to make her duties as a dean lighter and an inadequate faculty often makes her help in teaching necessary.

It is likely also that institutional budgets provide funds for teaching but not for the personnel and administrative type of work which a dean does. In such cases the dean must teach in order to justify her salary.

Through a closer investigation of the cases in which the deans do not teach, the writer found that in coeducational institutions the reasons vary. Sometimes the cause lies in the conception of the function of the dean. The person holding the position may be qualified to teach or she may not, but in some colleges she is never regarded as a person connected with academic matters at first hand; she may be thought of as a matron, a social director, as a personnel worker, but never as a scholar and a teacher. In other institutions, particularly if small, the administration would like to have a dean who can teach, but not being able to get all the desirable qualities in one person, it contents itself with a person who will be a satisfactory dean and waives teaching duties. Again, in a small college, the dean may be qualified to teach but unable to do so because there is no vacancy on the faculty in her teaching subject. In the large coeducational institutions there are deans who, though they have won distinction as instructors and research workers, are obliged to give up teaching because of the stress of other tasks. They say they can not continue it in justice to the students in their classes, their own health, and the other duties to be performed. Voluntarily, but with regret, they renounce their classroom work. It was invariably found that when a dean of a college for women was not teaching, the cause lay in the burden of other duties and not in the view held concerning the office or in lack of qualification on the part of the dean.

It may be that the 28 per cent of the deans who are not teaching represent a trend in this vocation away from the dean as a specialist in a teaching subject toward the dean as a specialist in the duties peculiar to the dean's office. It may be that in five years the percentage of deans of all types who do not teach will be much larger because they will be concentrating on the work of their office. And this need not mean that the dean will become less scholarly. It only means that instead of doing research work

TABLE XI

NUMBER OF DEANS WHO TEACH

(263 CASES)

ITEM	GROUP I							
	Coed. (84 Cases)		W. I. (17 Cases)		W. A. (6 Cases)		Total (1.7 Cases)	
	No.	Per Cent	No.	Per Cent	No.	Per Cent	No.	Per Cent
Number of Replies ...	84	——	17	——	6	——	107	—
Teaching	60	71.4	12	70.5	3	50.0	75	70

ITEM	GROUP II (82 CASES)		GROUP III (74 CASES)		TOTAL ALL GROUPS (263 CASES)	
	No.	Per Cent	No.	Per Cent	No.	Per Cent
Number of Replies	82		74	—	263	——
Teaching........................	58	70.7	54	73	187	71.7

in English literature, history, or Latin, the scholarly dean will carry on work in some phase of college administration or personnel. It may be that as time goes on the vocational approach to a deanship, particularly in a coeducational institution, will be less often by way of teaching. As conditions are at present, however, the woman dean, in more than seven cases in ten, is a teacher.

Whether the dean in a given institution ought to teach in the present transitional stage of her vocation, no one can say who does not know the institution thoroughly. It might be that the institution would profit if some of the energy she is devoting to classes in freshman English were turned toward the solution of housing difficulties. On the other hand, the impetus given to student scholarship by a dean who is herself successfully engaged in the familiar type of teaching and studying may be exactly what students need most.

There are, however, some deans who stoutly maintain that the function of dean is of itself so important as not to need the support of any other field. They hold that the personnel and administrative work of their office needs all their energy, acumen, and time; that they should concentrate upon ministry to student needs and upon research as to ways and means of meeting such needs.

YEARLY SCHEDULE OF TEACHING

Not all deans who teach do so during each semester of the college year. Most colleges have two semesters of about 16 weeks each. During the first semester, 184 deans teach; during the second, 177. During the summer only 31 teach.

NUMBER OF HOURS PER WEEK TAUGHT BY DEANS

We have previously seen that the higher the academic standing of a college, the more likely it is to have a dean. The higher it is, the more likely it is to have a dean of superior educational advantages. From Table XII we get the additional information that the higher the rank of a college, the smaller the number of hours taught by the dean. For all groups in the first semester, when the greatest number are teaching, the range in hours per week is from one to 32; Q_1 is 4.28; the medium, 6.49; and Q_3, 10.43. The average number of hours for the first semester is 8.4; for the second, 8.12; and for the summer, 10.1. This, it must be remembered, does not include the time given to preparation, correction of papers, interviews, and personal research; it represents only the time spent in the classroom.

Koos,[1] in studying the teaching load of the faculty of the University of Washington, found that for all the work of an instructional character including time spent in class, preparation for class sessions, reading papers, and the supervision of student research, the average number of hours for seven deans was 22.9. To reach this amount it would be necessary for the women deans considered in this study, for whom the average number of hours per week during the first semester is 8.4, to spend on their teaching outside the classroom 14.5 hours per week. This would be a large amount for persons who have such manifold duties and who are not for the most part academic deans as are most of those considered by Koos.

The standardization of the number of hours taught by deans would be very difficult because of the many variables involved. Some of these are: the dean's experience or lack of experience in teaching; the subject taught; the nature of the work, elementary or advanced; the type of teaching, whether lecture, laboratory, or recitation; the number of sections in the same subject; assistance in marking papers; the amount of other work done by the dean; fatigue resulting from other work.

Common sense should set some minimum standards which would prevent a college from expecting a dean in an institution with more than a thousand students to teach twenty hours per week and also supervise the social life of the women students. If common sense does not prevail, then an outside standardizing agency which could prevent such a situation would benefit the students, the dean, the college—indeed, the whole cause of higher education.

SUBJECTS TAUGHT BY WOMEN DEANS

As we have intimated before, the woman dean was a teacher before she was a dean. She chose her teaching subject many years before she even thought of becoming a dean. She chose it on the basis of her own academic interests, or for some less sensible reason, taught it for a time, and, because she showed certain qualifications for the work of dean, she was officially appointed to the position in the institution in which she was teaching. Sometimes she retained her teaching duties in addition to her

[1] Koos, Leonard. U. S. Bureau of Education, Bulletin, 1919, No. 15, p. 23.

TABLE XII

HOURS PER WEEK OF TEACHING BY WOMEN DEANS FIRST AND SECOND
SEMESTER AND SUMMER SESSION

(187 CASES)

| MEASURE | GROUP I | | | | | | | | | | |
| | Coed. | | | W. I. | | | W. A. | | | All Schools | |
	*1	**2	†SS	*1	**2	†SS	*1	**2	†SS	*1	**2
Q₁	2.31	3.31	5.25	2.95	2.60	—	2.25	2.25	—	3.12	3.02
Median	5.44	5.71	9.00	4.00	3.30	—	6.00	6.00	—	5.39	6.38
Q₃	7.69	7.33	17.63	6.17	6.25	—	8.75	8.75	—	7.50	7.25

| MEAS-URE | GROUP I All Schools †SS | GROUP II | | | GROUP III | | | ALL SCHOOLS COMBINED | | |
		*1	**2	†SS	*1	**2	†SS	*1	**2	†SS
Q₁	5.25	5.13	4.75	5.17	5.60	5.65	4.00	4.28	3.86	5.05
Median	9.00	8.67	8.20	8.50	9.50	9.25	8.00	6.49	6.45	8.37
Q₃	17.63	11.86	11.55	15.00	13.75	13.25	12.00	10.43	10.23	15.35

* 1 = First Semester.
** 2 = Second Semester.
† SS = Summer Session.

work as dean; often she dropped a certain number of classes;
more rarely she gave up all teaching. In case she had been a
productive scholar she usually ceased to be so from the moment
she became dean. If she had academic rank, she retained it after
appointment if possible.

Whether or not the dean ought to be a teacher as well as dean,
the fact remains that the most usual road at present to the deanship is a teaching position. This being so, a young woman who
plans to become a dean would like to know which teaching subjects, if any, will lead her most naturally into the deanship. The
answer to her question must come from an examination of the
academic histories of deans now in service.

It was found that the 187 deans previously discussed teach
thirty-five different subjects. One hundred fifty-seven deans, or
84 per cent, teach only one subject; twenty-six teach two sub-

jects more or less closely related, such as French and German; one teaches three; and one teaches four. The four subjects occurring most frequently in the group—English, history, Latin, and French—belong to the liberal arts. The vocational subjects, education and home economics, which are younger in the educational world, come next in frequency. The sciences are very sparsely represented.

From the point of view of college administration certain teaching subjects are probably more desirable for deans than are others. It is easier, for example, to fit a dean into a department of English. For one thing, this department can assimilate a woman with considerable ease. Secondly, it requires more teachers than any other department. Again, it is probably advisable for a dean to choose a teaching subject of which matter and method vary little from year to year rather than a subject that develops more rapidly. One dean, a Doctor of Philosophy, with several years of study abroad to her credit, told the writer that her status in the university in which she serves would be much improved if she were teaching, but that so much new material had been added recently to her teaching subject that she could not find time to "catch up" and she chose to do no teaching rather than to do it poorly. If the amount of time which deans can spend on study and research in their teaching subject is so small that prospective deans can not choose certain teaching subjects or certain specialists can not become deans, there is bound to be in time a reduction in the number of deans who are teachers or else a concentration in certain fields of subject matter.

Looking at the matter from another point of view, the college administrator choosing a dean may well ask, "Is there a relation between the personality of the woman who chooses a certain subject because she is most interested in it and the woman who possesses the temperamental qualifications necessary for a dean? Is a woman with a *penchant* for English literature more likely to be attracted to the work of a dean and to succeed in it inasmuch as human relationships figure largely in both? Many teachers of mathematics are casting wistful eyes at deanships. Is it, one wonders, because they feel their work too abstract and remote from college youth in whom they are genuinely interested, or is it because they are hindered from advancing in mathematics by competition with men, since men more often than women are

TABLE XIII

SUBJECTS TAUGHT BY WOMEN DEANS (187 CASES)

SUBJECT	CLASSIFICATION OF INSTITUTIONS						TOTAL ALL GROUPS
	GROUP I				Group II	Group III	
	Coed.	W. I.	W. A.	Total			
Art	1	–	1	2	–	–	2
Bible	–	–	–	–	2	1	3
Biology	1	–	–	1	–	–	1
Botany	–	–	–	–	1	–	1
Chemistry	–	–	–	–	–	1	1
Economics	2	–	–	2	–	–	2
Education	7	–	–	7	4	4	15
English	20	1	1	22	14	21	57
Ethics	–	–	–	–	–	1	1
French	2	–	–	2	8	6	16
German	1	–	–	1	4	3	8
Government	–	1	–	1	–	–	1
Greek	–	1	–	1	2	2	5
History	5	5	–	10	5	6	21
Home Economics	3	–	–	3	4	3	10
Hygiene	2	1	–	3	3	1	7
Latin	6	1	–	7	5	5	17
Library	–	–	–	–	2	–	2
Mathematics	3	–	1	4	5	–	9
Mental Hygiene	1	–	–	1	–	–	1
Nature Study	1	–	–	1	–	–	1
Orientation for Freshman	–	1	–	1	–	2	3
Philosophy	1	–	–	1	–	2	3
Physical Education	–	–	–	–	1	1	2
Piano	–	–	–	–	–	1	1
Political Science	–	–	–	–	1	1	2
Psychology	1	–	–	1	1	1	3
Public Speaking	1	–	–	1	–	–	1
Religious Education	1	–	–	1	–	1	2
Social Usage	–	–	–	–	1	1	2
Sociology	3	1	–	4	1	1	6
Spanish	–	–	–	–	2	1	3
Speech	–	–	–	–	–	1	1
Vocational Guidance	2	–	–	2	4	1	7
Vocations for Women	–	–	–	–	1	1	2
Voice	1	–	–	1	–	–	1

chosen for the more important posts in mathematics? We need research on the matter. It would help very much in the selection of deans to know whether an excellent mathematician is likely to be an excellent dean of any type, whether she is likely to make an excellent academic dean and a poor social dean, or whether there is no correlation between success in mathematics and success as a dean. It is also highly desirable to put to the test the old conjecture that a teacher of a cultural subject, such as Greek, is likely to have a "more genteel influence on the young ladies," than, let us say, a teacher of pure science.

When it comes to a study of the practical bearing of information gained in the teaching subject to the actual work of a dean, little help can be gained from the testimony of the deans themselves. There is bound to be a tendency on the part of each dean to emphasize the phase of her work most closely related to her preparation and previous experience. The only way in which to get a perspective on the matter is to study what a majority of deans actually do in order to see which subjects in the college curriculum bear most directly on what they do. In trying to establish the relationship, one must keep in mind the fact that to a certain degree what a dean does is influenced by what she is prepared to do. Some conclusions on the subject are given in Chapter XII, Vocational Guidance for Prospective Deans, which is based on the analysis of duties in Chapter XI.

SUMMARY

In this chapter we have considered the dean as a teacher. We have found that 70 per cent of the 263 deans studied are now teaching. The proportion of those who teach appears to be about the same in all types of institutions, in coeducational schools and in women's colleges, in colleges and universities of highest academic standing and in those of lowest. The fact is, though the figures in the tables do not show it, deans like to teach.

The range in hours of teaching per week among 187 deans is from 1 to 32. There appears to be a tendency for the dean to teach a smaller number of hours per week, the higher the rank of the institution which she serves. The medium number of hours per week is slightly over 6.

Such a teaching load, amounting to almost half that of the full-time college teacher, is too great to be imposed upon a woman who already has a full-time job as dean. Fortunately it probably represents only a temporary condition, a phase in the evolution of the dean's work from an avocation to a profession.

The spread of the subjects taught by deans is wide, thirty-six different subjects being taught by 187 deans. Eighty-four per cent of the deans teach only one subject. The subjects most often taught in order are English, history, Latin, French, education, and home economics. It would appear, therefore, that specializing in a given teaching subject has little relation to election of the vocation of dean.

CHAPTER VII

PREVIOUS EXPERIENCE OF DEANS

TYPES OF PREVIOUS EXPERIENCE

Seventy-one per cent of the 263 deans studied, we have noted in Chapter VI, are now teaching in addition to performing the duties of deans. Of this number 81 per cent were teachers before they were deans. For the 107 in Group I, the percentage is 79. Of these 107, 50 per cent were teachers in colleges before they were deans, 36 per cent had at some time taught in high schools, 5 per cent in normal schools, 6 per cent in elementary schools, and 5 per cent in private schools.

The returns for all groups showed twenty different types of experience in schools and colleges represented among the 263 deans studied. Fourteen had been principals of elementary schools; 12 had been high school principals; and 10, heads of school dormitories.

Sixty-seven deans, or 25 per cent, of the 263 had had professional experience not connected with schools. Thirty types of professional work are represented, those occurring most frequently being secretarial work in which 8 persons were engaged, social work with 8, and service for the Young Women's Christian Association with 12.

The data seem to indicate that women deans in colleges are recruited chiefly from the teaching profession and are most often teachers in colleges before they become deans.

PREVIOUS EXPERIENCE AS DEANS

For a position so important as that of dean one might expect that often previous experience as dean would be a requirement for appointment. As a matter of fact, we do find from Table XV that the higher the academic standing of the college, the greater the number of those having had previous experience in a deanship. Among the deans in all groups, however, only 59,

39

TABLE XIV

PREVIOUS EXPERIENCE AS DEAN, ASSISTANT DEAN, ASSISTANT TO THE DEAN
(90 Cases)*

TYPE OF EXPERIENCE	FREQUENCY			Total No.	All Groups Per Cent
	Group I No.	Group II No.	Group III No.		
Dean					
College or University	32	11	16	59	22.4
Normal School	3	2	4	9	3.4
High School	4	7	5	16	6.1
Assistant Dean					
College or University	9	1	5	15	5.7
Normal School	1	–	–	1	.4
High School	–	–	2	2	.8
Assistant to the Dean					
College or University	5	1	8	14	5.3
Normal School	–	–	–	–	–
High School	2	–	1	3	1.1
Total	56	22	41	119*	

* We note that 119 positions connected with a deanship are distributed among 90 persons.

TABLE XV

PERSONS WITH PREVIOUS EXPERIENCE CONNECTED WITH DEANSHIP
(263 Cases)

	FREQUENCY			Total	Per Cent
	Group I	Group II	Group III		
Persons with Experience ...	42	20	28	90	34.2
Persons without Experience .	65	62	46	173	65.8
Total	107	82	74	263	100.0

or 22 per cent, had experience as college deans before taking their present positions. Only 90 persons, or 34 per cent, had any experience connected with a deanship, such as dean, assistant dean, or assistant to the dean in college, normal, or high school before taking their present position.

We can account for this partly by the newness of the vocation and by the fact that the dean has so often been selected from the teaching corps of the institution in which she served. We can note that there is little tendency to go from a deanship in a normal school or high school to a deanship in a college.

Total Years of Experience Before Deanship

Only in the case of the deans in Group I was the writer able to ascertain the total number of years of other professional experience before appointment as dean in a college. Of the 107 deans in Group I, ten did not reply to the question. Among the remaining 97, the range in years is from none to 27. Only one person answering, however, had had no other experience as a wage-earner before she became a dean. Q_1 for all colleges was 6.5; the median 10.6; Q_3, 17.2. It is worth noting that the number of years of previous professional experience is in general higher among the deans in women's colleges—independent and affiliated—than among deans in coeducational colleges. Apparently for these positions in which, as we shall see in Chapter X, the duties differ from those of the dean in a coeducational college, women of longer experience are chosen.

Estimated Age of Deans

It would have been desirable to have included in this study an investigation of the age of deans. No such inquiry was made, however, since women are notoriously reticent on the subject and it was desired not to arouse inhibitions by asking for information on this subject. Some light can be obtained, however, from a scrutiny of the years of previous experience. From these figures we can get some indication of the age of the deans in this group at the time of appointment to their first deanships. The normal age for graduation from college is 22. If we add to this the figure showing median number of years of other professional experience, we may estimate the age at first appointment to a deanship, as median, 32.6 (Q_1 is 28.5, and Q_3, 39.2) which would indicate that 50 per cent of the deans were between 28 and 39 years when they became deans. A fourth of the group, it should be noted, are presumably less than 28 years old.

This method of computation, of course, does not take into consideration the deans who did not go to college at all or who went late in life. The result, however, appears to be in accord with the age specified in requests for nominations to deanships which the writer has examined.

TABLE XVI

Total Years of Wage-Earning Previous to Appointment as Dean

(107 Cases)

Measure	Group I			Total
	Coed.	W. I.	W. A.	
Q₁	6.1	10.25	7.5	6.5
Median	10.0	14.5	12.5	10.6
Q₃	16.0	21.75	19.5	17.25

Every request for a college dean coming to Teachers College of Columbia University for the last three years has specified, if it has mentioned age at all, "a woman of about thirty-five years." Thirty-five, it appears, is a magical age when a woman is old enough to have had experience in life and to have developed good judgment, but it is not too old to be in sympathy with youth or to adapt to a new situation.

Years in Present Position

The matter of tenure of office in this vocation is of great importance for the guidance of prospective deans. Persons who

TABLE XVII

Number of Years in Present Position

(263 Cases)

Measure	Group I	Group II	Group III	Total
Range	1–21	1–20	1–17	1.21
Q₁	2.0	1.2	1.4	1.7
Median	4.2	3.7	2.7	3.5
Q₃	7.7	7.3	5.1	6.9

make a college deanship their vocational aim should know the annual turnover in college deanships, and the length of time a dean usually holds her office. There seems to be a decided opinion among educators that the turnover in deanships is small, inasmuch

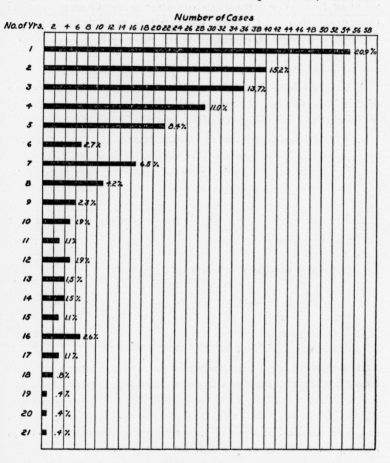

FIGURE II

YEARS OF EXPERIENCE IN PRESENT POSITION

as it is believed that the positions are among the more desirable ones open to women and that they are usually held by mature people who settle into deanships for the rest of their professional careers. The theory is not supported, however, by the data gathered for this study. Of the 263 deans noted, all but one stated how long she had been in her present position. The range in years is from 1 to 21; Q_1 is 1.7; the median is 3.5; and Q_3 is 6.9. Over one-fifth have been in their present positions only one year; approximately one-half have been in their present positions three years or less. The institutions of better academic standing hold their deans somewhat longer, but in all types of institutions the number of changes in deanships is surprisingly large.

SUMMARY

A separate investigation should be made regarding the cause of this brief service. From interviews with deans the writer has found that the following are often contributing factors:

1. The physical breakdown of deans due to
   a. The arduous nature of the duties.
   b. The fact that women, being comparatively new in administration, do not always use their strength to the best advantage.
2. The return of deans to purely teaching positions because they find they prefer teaching to administrative work.
3. The occasional influence of politics upon appointments to deanships in state and municipal institutions.
4. An increase in the number of openings for deans in coeducational institutions as a result of the post-war agitation about the social standards of the youth of the country.
5. The resignation during the last five years of a number of deans who had been in office for some time.

It is possible that the number of available positions as dean between 1921 and 1926 was larger than it will be again for some years. A study made by Professor Sarah M. Sturtevant of Teachers College in 1927 shows that, of the 392 deans replying in 1926 to Questionnaire I of this study, 46 resigned in the year 1926-1927, making the turnover 12 per cent for that year.

CHAPTER VIII

SALARIES OF WOMEN DEANS

The information available heretofore concerning the salaries paid to women deans in colleges and universities is so scanty and misleading that only the vaguest notions prevail concerning the remuneration received in this vocation. A young woman teaching in a college or university hears of a dean who receives $5,000 and thereupon thinks the vocation attractive financially. She does not hear, however, of the training and experience the dean has brought to the position nor has she any notion of the amount of money the dean must spend for living quarters, clothing, entertainment of guests, and incidental expenses peculiar to the position. Or this young person may hear of a dean who receives only $2,000 and may forthwith decide that she cannot afford to be a dean. She does not hear that the dean in addition to $2,000 in cash receives all living free of charge for herself and two children. She has no way of knowing the relative number of deans receiving $5,000 and $2,000, respectively, or the factors that tend to determine the salary in a given situation.

The Computation of the Salaries

In order to secure trustworthy information concerning salaries, the investigation included several questions on the point in Questionnaire III and Questionnaire IV. Each dean was asked to state: (1) her present salary in cash during the college year; (2) her present salary in cash during the summer session; (3) whether she regularly served as dean during the summer session; and (4) whether living was provided for her by the college.

Each of the deans in Group I was asked also: (1) whether she lived in a dormitory, and (2) whether she performed dormitory duties.

Of the 263 deans replying to the questionnaire, 7 did not give any information concerning salary and 6 who were in Cath-

45

olic institutions stated that theirs was "consecrated service," not even their living being considered remuneration. There were therefore 250 persons who stated their salaries.

In computing the salaries it was found necessary arbitrarily to determine the value of total living and partial living when provided by the institution. Deans who received total living as part of their salary were found to vary in their estimation of the value of the living from $200 to $1,200, each dean's evaluation being largely dependent upon the style and cost of living to which she was accustomed before appointment to the deanship. It was decided after consultation with various persons acquainted with the computation of salaries, to evaluate total living expenses when provided for any dean during the college year at $600; a room or rooms only, at $200; board only, at $400. Living during the summer was computed accordingly, when received, and added to total salary. If the dean was given living for members of her family it was computed at the same rate. If the college provided a house for the dean, the writer ascertained the amount of rent paid for a similar house in the community and computed the dean's salary accordingly.

Living Expenses Provided. One hundred twenty-five deans, or 50 per cent of those reporting salaries, received living from their institutions, which in Table XXII is included in the amount of

TABLE XVIII

WOMEN DEANS WITH LIVING EXPENSES PROVIDED

REMUNERATION OF DEAN	FREQUENCY						
	Group I				Group II	Group III	All Groups
	Coed.	W. I.	W. A.	Total			
All Living Expenses	35	10	2	47	33	45	125
Partial Living Expenses .	9	1	1	11	11	5	27
No Living Expenses	39	6	3	48	38	24	110
Unknown	1	—	—	1	—	—	1
Total Number of Deans .	84	17	6	107	82	74	263

TABLE XIX

SUMMER SERVICE AS DEAN

(263 Cases)

TYPE OF SERVICE	FREQUENCY						
	GROUP I				Group II	Group III	All Groups
	Coed.	W. I.	W. A.	Total			
Regular	14	0	0	14	21	10	45
Sometimes	0	0	1	1	1	4	6
None	70	17	5	92	60	60	212
Total Number of Deans .	84	17	6	107	82	74	263

TABLE XX

WOMEN DEANS IN DORMITORIES

(107 Cases)

ITEM	FREQUENCY			
	GROUP I			Total
	Coed.	W. I.	W. A.	
Living in Dormitory	35	9	2	46
Performing Dormitory Duties	28	5	0	33

total salary received. Twenty-seven, or 11 per cent, received partial living.

Service in Summer Session. In the case of 45 deans, or 18 per cent of those reporting salaries, the amount stated includes pay for service as dean during the summer session. Of the 23 deans of colleges for women in Group I (see Table XIX), only one serves in the summer, a fact which is explained by the small number of colleges for women which have a summer session.

Women Deans in Dormitories. Of the deans in Group I, 46,

or 17 per cent of those reporting salaries, live in dormitories and of these 33, or 72 per cent, perform dormitory duties. The performance of these duties is significant in the consideration of salary. The living received by a dean who resides in a dormitory is sometimes regarded as so much additional salary easily acquired, but comments written by deans on their questionnaires indicate that the living so obtained is laboriously earned. A number of deans said, "I prefer to forego the living thus provided and reside off-campus."

DISCUSSION OF THE SALARIES RECEIVED

The lowest salary found in the group studied was $400. This was received by the dean of women in a coeducational institution. Another low-paid deanship was in a nonaccredited coeducational college in which a student in the junior class holds the title and performs the duties of dean of women for tuition and living. Only fifteen persons, it may be noted, receive a salary over $5,000, and of these fourteen are in institutions of highest academic rank. The one dean in Group II receiving a salary over $5,000 was dean of home economics and dean of women in an agricultural college. In Group III, which is composed of nonaccredited institutions, there is no salary over $3,999. The highest salary is $11,700, received by the dean of an affiliated college for women, who is practically a college president. The median in all institutions is $2,766.60; Q_1 is $2,096.40; and Q_3 is $3,531.80.

With these figures it is interesting to compare those cited by T. T. Chung in his Doctor's dissertation, entitled, *Personnel Study of Teachers in Colleges, Universities, and Normal Schools,* which is a study of persons placed during nine months in positions by the Bureau of Educational Service of Teachers College, Columbia University. His findings with reference to the salaries of women appointed to teach in colleges are as follows:

TYPE OF TEACHER	NUMBER OF CASES	RANGE IN SALARY	MEDIAN SALARY
College, Full Professor	27	$1,500–14,250	$2,328
University, Full Professor	7	2,000–13,600	2,886
College, All Other Ranks	100	1,000– 3,500	2,119
University, All Other Ranks	63	1,000– 3,600	2,245

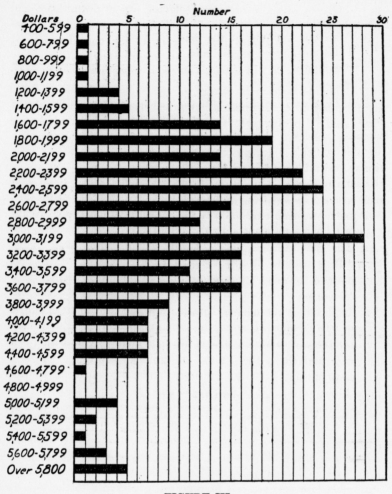

FIGURE III
Salaries of 250 Deans

The medium salary for the women appointed by Teachers College to full professorships in universities is $119.40 more than the median salary of the deans studied from all three groups.

Factors Related to the Amount of Salary

Some factors apparently related to the amount of salary paid to a woman dean in a college or university are as follows:

1. Type of institution (coeducational or for women only).
2. Academic standing of the institution.
3. Academic training of the dean.
4. Total enrollment of students.
5. Enrollment, if the institution is coeducational, of women students.

The Type of Institution. Of the 250 institutions in which the salary of the dean is known, 163 are coeducational and 87 are women's colleges. The upper limit of the first quartile ($1,950) for the women's colleges is $161.60 less than that for the coeducational institution ($2,111.60). From that point on, however, the salaries appear to be better in the women's colleges than those paid in coeducational institutions.

Possible reasons explaining why deans in colleges for women appear to be better paid are these:

1. The dean in a women's college is usually dean of the entire college and is usually thought to have a more important position academically and administratively than that of dean of women.
2. In a college for women, all expenditures are made on behalf of the women, whereas in a coeducational institution, the interests of women students are in competition with those of men and the salary of the dean of women may suffer in consequence.

TABLE XXI

SALARIES OF WOMEN DEANS IN COEDUCATIONAL COLLEGES AND UNIVERSITIES AND IN COLLEGES FOR WOMEN

MEASURE	TYPE OF INSTITUTION	
	COED.	WOMEN'S
Q_1	$2,111.60	$1,950.00
Median	2,678.60	3,200.00
Q_3	3,350.00	4,050.00

The Academic Standing of the Institution. Table XXII shows that the higher the academic standing of the college, the higher the salary of the dean is likely to be. The range of salary in

TABLE XXII

SALARIES OF WOMEN DEANS (263 Cases)

(Frequency Table According to Academic Standing of Institutions)

SALARY	GROUP I	GROUP II	GROUP III	TOTAL
Consecrated Service	1	3	2	6
Unknown	3	1	3	7
$ 400– 599	—	1	—	1
600– 799	—	1	—	1
800– 999	—	—	1	1
1,000–1,199	—	—	1	1
1,200–1,399	1	1	2	4
1,400–1,599	—	3	2	5
1,600–1,799	2	4	8	14
1,800–1,999	1	5	13	19
2,000–2,199	—	7	7	14
2,200–2,399	5	8	9	22
2,400–2,599	3	9	12	24
2,600–2,799	4	8	3	15
2,800–2,999	7	4	1	12
3,000–3,199	16	10	2	28
3,200–3,399	11	3	2	16
3,400–3,599	4	3	4	11
3,600–3,799	11	4	1	16
3,800–3,999	7	1	1	9
4,000–4,199	6	1	—	7
4,200–4,399	4	3	—	7
4,400–4,599	6	1	—	7
4,600–4,799	1	—	—	1
4,800–4,999	—	—	—	—
5,000–5,199	4	—	—	4
5,200–5,399	2	—	—	2
5,400–5,599	1	—	—	1
5,600–5,799	2	1	—	3
5,800–5,999	—	—	—	—
6,000–6,199	1	—	—	1
6,200–6,399	—	—	—	—
6,400–6,599	—	—	—	—
6,600–6,799	2	—	—	2
6,800–6,999	—	—	—	—
7,000–7,199	—	—	—	—
7,200–7,399	—	—	—	—
7,400–7,599	1	—	—	1
7,600–7,799	—	—	—	—
11,700	1	—	—	1
Total	107	82	74	263

colleges and universities in Group I is from $1,200 to $11,700; in Group II, from $400 to $5,600; in Group III from $800 to $3,800.

For salaries in institutions of Group I, Q_1 is $2,992.80; the median is $3,391.60; Q_3 is $5,141.50. In Group II, Q_1 is $2,042.80; the median is $2,555.60; Q_3 is $3,130.00. In Group III, Q_1 is $1,787.60; the median is $2,142.80; Q_3 is $2,525.00.

The Academic Training of the Dean. Table XXIV indicates that the higher the academic training of the dean, the higher the salary she is likely to receive, except for the first quartile of persons with the Doctor's degree. Among those with only the Bachelor's degree, Q_1 is $1,704.60; among those with the Master's

TABLE XXIII

SUMMARY

SALARIES OF WOMEN DEANS ACCORDING TO ACADEMIC STANDING OF INSTITUTIONS STUDIED

(250 Cases)

MEASURE	CLASSIFICATION OF INSTITUTIONS			TOTAL
	Group I	Group II	Group III	
Range	$1,200–11,700	$400–5,600	$800–3,800	$400–11,700
Q_1	2,992.80	2,042.80	1,787.60	2,096.40
Median	3,391.60	2,555.60	2,142.80	2,766.60
Q_3	5,141.60	3,130.00	2,525.00	3,531.80

degree, Q_3 is $2,420.60, or $716 more. The median salary of those deans with only a Bachelor's degree is $2,483.40; the median salary of those with the Master's degree is $438.80 more, or $2,922.20; and the median salary of those with the doctorate is $427.80 more than that of the deans with the Master's degree. Q_3 in the case of persons with only the Bachelor's degree is $3,262.60; in the case of persons with the Master's degree is $245.80 more, or $3,508.40; the median salary of persons holding the Doctor's degree is $958.20 more, or $4,466.60. The figures referring to persons with no degree lose significance when we observe how much training these deans have often had in a special line, such as music, which has not led to a conventional degree.

Salary in Relation to Total Enrollment of Students. Both total enrollment of students and salary of the dean were obtained from two hundred institutions. The data presented in Table XXV indicate that the larger the total enrollment of students the larger the salary of the dean tends to be. The coefficient of correlation between salary and total enrollment in women's colleges is .43; between salary and total enrollment in coeducational institutions it is .63.

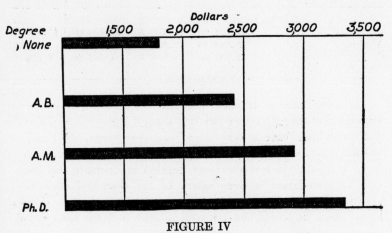

FIGURE IV

SALARIES AND DEGREES OF DEANS OF WOMEN

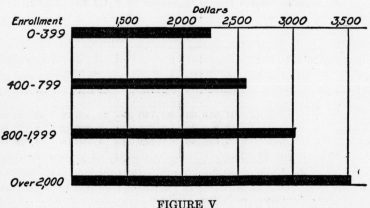

FIGURE V

SALARIES AND ENROLLMENTS

54 *A Personnel Study of Women Deans*

TABLE XXIV

SALARIES OF WOMEN DEANS ACCORDING TO DEGREES HELD

(250 Cases)

Measure	Degree			
	A.B.	A.B. and A.M. or A.M. Only	Ph.D.	No Degree
Q_1	$1,704.60	$2,420.60	$2,400.00	$1,450.00
Median	2,483.40	2,922.20	3,350.00	1,833.40
Q_3	3,262.60	3,508.40	4,466.60	2,250.00

The Enrollment of Women in Coeducational Institutions. The writer found through interviews that though a given coeducational institution may have a very large total enrollment, the dean of women may receive a small salary if the number of women students is small. It was therefore decided to calculate the coefficient of correlation between salary of the dean and enrollment of women in coeducational institutions. This is .69, slightly higher than the coefficient between salaries and the total enrollment of students in the same institutions.

TABLE XXV

SALARIES OF WOMEN DEANS ACCORDING TO TOTAL ENROLLMENT

Measure	Number of Students Enrolled			
	Under 399	400–799	800–1,999	2,000 and Over
Q_1	$1,959.00	$2,140.00	$2,500.00	$3,158.40
Median	2,269.20	2,575.00	3,028.60	3,575.00
Q_3	2,635.80	3,225.00	3,750.00	4,250.00

COEFFICIENT OF CORRELATION BETWEEN SALARY AND OTHER FACTORS

1. Total Enrollment in Women's colleges .... .428
2. Total Enrollment in Coeducational Institutions .... .627
3. Total Enrollment of Women in Coeducational Institutions .... .686

SUMMARY

Six per cent of the 250 deans reporting receive over $5,000. Q_1 is $2,096.40; the median is $2,766.60; Q_3 is $3,531.80. In the case of 152, or 61 per cent, of the deans reporting, these figures include partial or total living expenses, computed at a uniform rate. Fifty per cent receive all their living; 11 per cent have partial living. Forty-six deans, or 18 per cent, of 250 reporting from all groups live in dormitories; 33, or 13 per cent of 107 reporting from Group I, must perform dormitory duties in return for their living. In the case of 45, or 18 per cent of the 250 deans, the salary quoted entails service as dean during the summer session.

Five pronounced trends can be seen in the salaries quoted:

1. The higher the academic standing of an institution, the higher the salary of the dean.
2. The higher the academic training of the dean, the higher her salary.
3. The larger the enrollment of students in an institution, the higher the salary of the dean.
4. The larger the total enrollment of women students in a co-educational institution, the higher the salary of the dean.
5. Salaries of deans in colleges for women tend to be larger than for deans of women in coeducational institutions.

CHAPTER IX

SOCIAL RELATIONSHIPS

Academic study, professional training, and experience are not the only factors in the vocational experience of a woman which are scrutinized before her appointment to a deanship. Her family status and religion may in some cases be determining factors in regard to her election.

The Family Status of Deans

In the bulletin of the Carnegie Foundation for the Advancement of Teaching, "The Professional Preparation of Teachers for American Public Schools" (Number Fourteen, 1920, pp. 139-143), it is strongly urged that women teachers continue their work after marriage. Some persons believe that for the work of dean, marriage and motherhood are highly desirable. Certain educators who are ordinarily loath to see a married woman in a profession, feel strongly that a woman dean, particularly if she is to deal with social problems, should have been married, and that it is highly desirable that she shall have reared children of her own. She will, according to the argument, understand young people better and will be listened to with more respect than a spinster because she has had the experience of romance and marriage to which the students in her charge are looking forward. "She should," maintains one professor of sociology, "get her Doctor's degree while young, marry early, and have several boys and girls before assuming deanship." He does not decree at what age she should become a dean or how her family are to be provided for when she does.

Other persons who have observed the deanship from the sociological and psychological points of view, in refutation of the theory of the desirability of marriage for the vocation, point to the superlatively fine work done by unmarried deans. Marriage in itself, they say, does not give women constructive imagination with regard to life problems of young women nor does failure to marry mean that a woman is incapable of understanding the romantic element of life. Believers in sublimation maintain further that these women have found in the work a desirable redirection of sex energy. So much has been said on the subject and with such emotional emphasis that we look with interest to see the number of deans in Group I who are married.

TABLE XXVI
FAMILY STATUS OF DEANS IN GROUP I
(107 Cases)

STATUS	NUMBER	PER CENT
Married	26	24.3
Unmarried	81	75.7

From Table XXVI we see that 81, or 76 per cent, are unmarried and 26, or 24 per cent, are married. Of the 26 who are married, 19 are widowed. Of the 19 widows, 9 have at least one dependent and 3 have at least one partial dependent, making a total of 12 widows with dependents. No married woman in the group who is not a widow has dependents; therefore the total number of married women with dependents is 12, or 45 per cent. Ten of the unmarried deans have dependents. Five have at least one person who is totally dependent, and five have at least one partially dependent, making 12 per cent of the unmarried deans with dependents. Of all the deans answering in this group, 26 per cent have dependents. Twenty-five deans, or 24 per cent, have relatives living with them.

In fifteen investigations of the number of women wage-earners "with dependents" [1] more than one-half of the women reported that they had dependents. In twenty other studies, more than 40 per cent reported that they had dependents. The per cent of the whole group was 41.3. The conclusion was drawn that about two-fifths of the wage-earning women questioned "feel a definite responsibility for the entire or partial support of one or more dependents." Deans in Group I apparently have less responsibility of this kind than a group of miscellaneous wage-earning women.

[1] "The Share of Wage-Earning Women in Family Support." U. S. Department of Labor. *Bulletin of the Women's Bureau*, No. 30, 1923, p. 170.

It is impossible to tell whether the small number of married deans in these colleges of highest rank is due to the fact that stress is not laid upon marriage as a qualification or because married women with other desirable qualifications for the work are not available. Among the files of two placement offices the writer rarely found specific requests for married deans. Officials probably realize that mothers who take up the work of a deanship in middle life when there are fewer responsibilities in their own homes may or may not make a satisfactory adjustment or readjustment to college life. Such women sometimes find that the ability to rear children of their own in admirable fashion does not mean that they understand the modern flapper or can deal with large groups of girls. As for the young married women—those who leave deanships for marriage frequently do not wish to return to the work unless forced to by economic pressure. Again, when they would like to continue the work or resume it after a few years, sometimes they can not make adequate arrangements for their families during the hours when they must be out of their homes. It may be that as society makes better provision for the professional woman's family we shall have more married deans.

Church Affiliation of Deans

In this day of increasing tolerance in regard to religion, the matter of the church affiliation of a dean may seem irrelevant in a discussion of her qualifications. It is sometimes, however, of importance to her chances of election to a deanship.

A comparison of the type of control of the 107 colleges considered in Group I with the church membership of the dean in each of these colleges, shows that the nonsectarian colleges tend to have deans from a wide range of church membership while denominational colleges tend to choose deans who are members of the churches controlling the colleges. Even institutions, which were once denominational and are now alleged to be nonsectarian, show in the choice of a dean the effect of their former church control. It may be argued, of course, that the president of a Methodist college, for example, selects a Methodist dean not because she is a Methodist, but because he has among his acquaintances more persons who are Methodists. Doubtless this is often true. On the other hand, requests for nominations to deanships show that a denominational college prefers, other things being equal, a dean of its own sect.

TABLE XXVII

RELIGIOUS CONTROL OF INSTITUTIONS AND CHURCH AFFILIATIONS OF WOMEN DEANS

(107 Cases)

RELIGIOUS CONTROL OF INSTITUTIONS	No. of Institutions	CHURCH MEMBERSHIPS OF WOMEN DEANS													
		Baptist	Catholic	Community	Congregational	Disciple	Episcopal	Evangelical	Lutheran	Methodist	Non-Church	Presbyterian	Unitarian	Unknown	Total
Baptist*	3	2	—	—	—	—	1	—	—	—	—	—	—	—	3
Catholic	1	—	1	—	—	—	—	—	—	—	—	—	—	—	1
Congregational	1	—	—	—	1	—	—	—	—	—	—	—	—	—	1
Disciple	1	—	—	—	—	1	—	—	—	—	—	—	—	—	1
Evangelical	1	—	—	—	—	—	—	1	—	—	—	—	—	—	1
Lutheran	2	—	—	—	—	—	—	—	2	—	—	—	—	—	2
Methodist	11	—	—	—	2	—	—	—	—	9	—	—	—	—	11
Nonsectarian	76	6	—	1	21	—	14	—	—	10	6	10	3	3	76
Presbyterian	11	—	—	—	1	—	1	—	2	1	—	8	—	—	11
Total	107	8	1	1	25	1	16	1	4	20	6	18	3	3	107

* Read line thus: Of 3 institutions under Baptist control, two have Baptist deans, and one, an Episcopalian.

CHAPTER X

ANALYSIS OF DUTIES PERFORMED BY DEANS

We have noted in previous chapters certain trends in the vocation of dean toward a uniformity in matters such as academic preparation, rank, and remuneration. It is highly desirable to know whether there is also a tendency toward uniformity in the work performed by deans.

It is manifestly impossible to discover all the duties performed by deans. So diversified are the tasks that one dean may be personally running the oil heater in a dormitory while another dean in a different institution is appointing to the faculty a scholar of note as head of a new department. One, a physician, is found making physical examination of students; another, formerly a dietitian, supervises the food in a dormitory; a third, once the head of a vocational bureau, gives expert vocational advice; a fourth spends much time in working over the financial budget of her college.

Interesting though it might be to observe these variations in duties, we shall find it more profitable to concentrate on the uniformities, noting the duties that are performed by most deans and the frequency with which the most common duties are performed by each dean.

The method used in compiling the list of the dean's duties has been described in Chapter II. The results of the investigations can be seen in Chapter X. The data are presented in three subdivisions because, as the writer discovered quickly from interviews and questionnaires, the institutions in which these deans served are of three distinct types. There is the independent institution attended by men and women, e.g., Cornell University and the University of Chicago; the independent college for women, e.g., Vassar and Mt. Holyoke; and the college for women affiliated with other colleges in a university, e.g., Barnard College and Western Reserve College for Women.

Certain institutions ordinarily classed as universities for men, e.g., Harvard and Yale, are grouped with the coeducational institutions since they have women graduate students with a woman adviser; on the other hand, Radcliffe, although it is affiliated with Harvard, is grouped with the independent colleges for women because it has its own president to whom the dean is responsible.

Although the groups of the independent colleges for women and the affiliated colleges are not large enough to be significant statistically, they have to be considered as types of institutions into which deans must fit.

It is to be regretted that the detailed investigation of duties had to be restricted to institutions in Group I and could not be extended to each of the 263 colleges reporting a woman dean. So intensive an investigation, however, was not possible for so large a number. The writer can only point out the evidences of a trend toward uniformity in duties within the members of Group I and conclude that the colleges in Groups II and III are consciously or unconsciously tending toward the same goal.

Extraneous Functions Performed by Deans

Before discussing the duties which deans perform, we may consider what other functions besides that of dean they have in the institutions in which they serve. Two functions we have already noted; viz., teaching, which is performed by 70 per cent of deans in Group I, and dormitory service, performed by 30 per cent.

Twenty-eight, or 25 per cent, of the deans, we note from Table XXVIII, are in charge of at least one other important department of work. Ten, it appears, are heads of departments of a teaching subject, seven have charge of the placement of women students in permanent positions; one is in charge of vocational guidance; five are doing all or a part of the work ordinarily done by a registrar. One has as subdivisions of her office the bureaus of admissions, records, and vocational guidance, though each has its own immediate head. One has been publicity representative of the college. One is college physician and one acts as executive secretary of the graduate school.

In the affiliated colleges only one of the six deans performs one of the extra functions listed. Ten of the 16 deans in independent colleges perform one of the functions, and 15 of the 84 in coeducational institutions perform one.

Five factors which may require one person to perform one or more functions in addition to the duties ordinarily delegated to the dean are:

1. The form of organization of the institution.
2. The number and character of the students.
3. The relations between functions performed.
4. The abilities and interests of the dean.
5. The number of assistants provided.

TABLE XXVIII

EXTRANEOUS FUNCTIONS PERFORMED BY DEANS

(107 Cases)

FUNCTION	Coed.	W. I.	W. A.	Total
Executive Secretary of Graduate School	1	—	—	1
Head of Admissions	—	1	—	1
Head of Dept. in Teaching Subject	8	1	1	10
Head of Records	—	1	—	1
Head of Vocational Guidance	—	1	—	1
Physician of College	—	1	—	1
Placement:				
Head	3	4	—	7
Supervisor	—	1	—	1
Registrar:				
Entire Work	1	1	—	2
Part of Work	1	2	—	3
Total	15	13	1	29

Note:—Some of these listings represent duplications on the part of individuals.

Differences in organization in the three types of institutions probably explain why the dean in an affiliated college performs more than one of the functions enumerated. The dean in such an institution is practically head of the entire organization and as such is not likely to assume responsibility for any single phase. The dean in the coeducational institution is less likely than the dean in the independent colleges for women to take on an additional function, for in the coeducational institution phases of work such as the regulation of admissions or the keeping of records are likely to be managed by a single bureau for men and women students without a separate subdivision for women students. It is easy to understand why at Vassar College, the dean, whose duties are almost entirely academic, should be responsible for admissions, records, and vocational guidance though each of these departments has its own immediate head, while at Cornell University, on the other hand, admissions and academic records are handled by men for both men and women.

In the Harvard Graduate School of Education the small number of women and their maturity and seriousness of purpose allow time for the adviser to perform the threefold function of dean, registrar, and director of placement. In this institution we find an excellent example of the way in which different types of work may dovetail each other. A knowledge of the academic history of students gained by the dean as registrar can be used to great advantage in dealing with problems of personnel and helping students to appropriate positions.

From the figures we see that a majority of deans must do something foreign to the duties narrowly regarded as appertaining to the dean. Seventy per cent teach; 30 per cent serve in connection with dormitories; others have charge of appointments, admissions, etc. In short, the figures indicate that many deans have to be persons of considerable versatility.

To be successful in several lines, a dean must have talent, training, and time for each. It is conceivable that a person may be an excellent registrar but unable to do personnel work; may be an excellent dean but have no flair for the work of publicity representative; a good dean and a good head of placement without an adequate number of assistants for the two posts. So difficult is it to find the combination of these essentials that it is not surprising that only a fourth of the deans questioned perform any one of the extraneous functions listed, barring teaching and dormitory duties.

DUTIES PERFORMED AS DEAN

The duties belonging to the function of dean are approached in this chapter from two angles:

1. What kinds of work are done by the majority of deans?
2. What duties require most time?

In order to ascertain what duties were performed, the investigator asked each dean to describe her relation to various college committees; to enumerate the members of her staff, to state whether she and her assistants perform certain duties listed; and to name the personnel records which she used. (See Questionnaire IV, Appendix.) The results are stated in this chapter. Certain quantitative measurements of each dean's work were attempted through questions asked the dean and through a time-study of the work of two deans for a stated period. Results are given in Chapter XI.

THE DEAN'S RELATION TO COMMITTEES

The fact that a dean is not a member of a given committee in a college does not mean necessarily that she is not engaged in the work occupying the attention of the committee. For example, though she may not be an official member of the committee on health she may be working very hard to promote the good health of students, coöperating cordially in the work of the committee. If, however, we have a definite statement that the dean is a member of a certain committee, we may safely assume that the work of the committee has a bearing on the duties of dean. Furthermore, her specific relation to a given committee is significant. It is illuminating to discover whether the dean is simply a member, an ex-officio member, a chairman, or an interested nonmember who is sometimes consulted.

Questionnaire IV of this investigation asks for such information in regard to eleven committees frequently found in institutions of higher learning. The dean in coeducational institutions is in 52 cases out of 60 a member of a faculty committee on student activities, and in 47 cases out of 63 cases, a member of the committee dealing with discipline. Moreover, she is in 35 out of 60 of these institutions of highest academic rank a member of the committee on scholarship. She is frequently in coeducational institutions a member of the committees on scholarship, health, and housing. In 26 of the 84 institutions the dean is chairman of a committee.

In the independent colleges for women the faculty committees on which the dean is found most frequently have to do with academic matters. Fourteen colleges have a committee on academic scholarships; in 13 the dean is a member. Fifteen have a committee on admissions; in 10 the dean is a member. Twelve have a committee on curriculum, in each case she is a member.

In all the six affiliated colleges for women there is a committee on academic scholarship, of which the dean is a member. In each

TABLE XXIX

Women Deans on Standing Faculty Committees (107 Cases)

Name of Committee in Institution	Number of Colleges Having Committees	Relation of Dean to Committee				
		Member Only	Ex-Officio	Chairman	Consulted	No Connection
COEDUCATIONAL INSTITUTION (84 CASES)						
Academic Scholarship*	69	30	5	—	7	27
Admissions	68	15	7	1	9	36
Curriculum	66	13	3	—	3	47
Degrees	38	9	—	—	—	37
Discipline	63	40	7	6	3	7
Finance or Budget	24	4	1	—	1	18
Health	43	26	4	3	3	7
Housing	37	19	3	7	2	3
Loans	53	17	6	3	11	16
Scholarships	55	24	6	3	5	17
Student Activities	60	38	11	3	1	7
WOMEN'S AFFILIATED (6 CASES)						
Academic Scholarship .	6	1	3	2	–	–
Admission	5	2	1	–	–	–
Curriculum	6	1	1	1	–	2
Degrees	4	4	2	1	–	–
Discipline	4	1	1	2	–	1
Finance of Budget	3	1	2	–	–	–
Health	2	2	–	–	–	–
Housing	2	2	–	–	–	–
Loans	3	–	1	1	1	–
Scholarships	4	–	1	2	1	–
Student Activities	5	–	2	2	–	1
WOMEN'S INDEPENDENT (17 CASES)						
Academic Scholarship .	13	5	5	3	1	–
Admissions	15	5	3	2	1	4
Curriculum	12	6	6	–	–	–
Degrees	5	–	3	–	–	–
Discipline	8	2	2	3	–	1
Finance or Budget	4	–	1	–	1	2
Health	9	3	1	2	1	2
Housing	4	1	–	3	–	–
Loans	8	1	2	2	1	2
Scholarships	13	3	–	5	–	5
Student Activities	9	3	1	2	1	2

* Read first line thus: Sixty-nine of the 84 coeducational institutions have a committee on academic scholarship. In 30 the dean is merely a member; in 5 she is an ex-officio member; in 7 she is not a member but is consulted; and in 27 she has no contact with the committee.

of the four colleges having a committee on discipline she is a member of the committee, and in four cases out of five she is a member of the committee on student activities. In three out of five cases, she is a member of the committee on admissions; in three out of six on curriculum; in three out of four on degrees.

Summary. From an examination of these data concerning the dean's relation to faculty committees we may make the following observations:

1. Of each of the committees noted, except that on degrees, at least one dean from each of the three types is a member. To a limited extent the deans in the three types are concerned with the same problems.

2. The deans in colleges for women—independent and allied— are more frequently represented on committees dealing with academic matters than are deans in coeducational institutions, though there appears to be a trend toward giving the dean in the latter a voice in academic councils.

3. The dean in the coeducational institution is vitally concerned, if we may judge by representation on faculty committees, with student activities and discipline.

Assistants of Women Deans

An investigation of deans soon discloses the fact that there is another position which has arisen within recent years—that of assistant dean or assistant to the dean. Assisting the deans whose work is here surveyed were found 362 assistants or an average of three to each dean. The assistant is usually next in authority to the dean and acts as dean in her absence. Most often the assistant dean is placed in immediate charge of some division or divisions of the dean's office, such as off-campus housing, sororities, or social affairs. The position of assistant to the dean does not usually carry such weighty responsibilities as does that of assistant dean.

In addition to those persons officially designated as assistants, many deans have other helpers who are designated as clerks, secretaries, stenographers, and the like. To one of these is often given the title "assistant to the dean."

The fact that a dean has no assistant for a particular type of work does not indicate that the dean has no connection with that work. She may be doing it unassisted. She may not have a head of residence or a head of hall as her assistant because she herself

TABLE XXX
STAFF OF WOMEN DEANS
(107 Cases)

ASSISTANTS MENTIONED IN QUESTIONNAIRES	NUMBER OF DEANS HAVING ASSISTANTS			
	Coed.	W. I.	W. A.	Total
1. Assistant Dean of Women	14	2	–	16
2. Assistant to the Dean	29	3	–	32
3. Heads of Halls (Not Sorority Houses)	54	8	6	68
4. Chaperons of Sorority Houses	30	–	–	30
5. Social Director	7	–	1	8
6. Paid Chaperons for Social Functions	8	2	1	11
7. Vocational Director	6	4	2	12
8. Dietitian	14	7	3	24
9. Housekeeper	31	5	3	39
10. Cafeteria Director	9	1	–	10
11. Clerical Workers	18	1	4	23
12. Secretary	40	–	4	44
13. Secretary of Religious Organizations	16	2	–	18

ASSISTANTS ADDED BY DEANS	Coed.	W.I.	W.A.	Total
Academic Deans of Classes	–	1	–	1
Advisers	9	–	–	9
Associate Dean	–	1	–	1
Controller	–	–	1	1
Dietitian and Housekeeper Combined	4	–	–	4
Dietitian and Cafeteria Director	–	–	1	1
Head of Admissions	–	–	1	1
Head of Residence	–	–	1	1
Inspector of Off-Campus Housing	1	1	–	2
Nurse	5	–	–	5
Personnel Director	1	–	–	1
Total				362

acts as head of the only dormitory on the campus. On the other hand, the presence of an assistant for a particular type of work indicates definitely that the dean has responsibility in connection with the work; hence we note with interest the number and types of assistants listed in Table XXX.

The data presented therein show that assistants to the dean may be engaged with dormitories, sororities, social activities, vocational guidance, admissions, health or personnel work. The findings are corroborated by an examination of Table XXXI, showing which of 49 duties are performed by deans, by their assistants, or by both dean and assistants.

From Table XXX we may conclude that the work done by assistants is related in many instances to the work done by committees on which deans serve. We also see that the types of work done by assistants are well distributed over the three types of institutions. To be sure, only one person, the dean of Barnard College, has directly under her a controller and a head of residence, but, in general, the assistants named in the three types of institutions are much the same. Only an intimate study of the organization of each institution would reveal how remote or how close the dean may be to the work of a given assistant. Item C in Table XXXI indicates what appears to be an important point in organization; *viz.,* that not often, even in coeducational institutions, are the dean and her assistants actually doing the same sort of work. In interviews with deans the writer learned that both deans and assistants prefer a rather sharp differentiation of duties. By such a plan the dean is able to delegate those phases of work for which by training and inclination she is least inclined to an assistant who is particularly gifted for that work. The assistant for her part is much more contented, especially if she is a person of initiative, originality, and energy, to have charge of specific lines of work in which she can feel herself an administrator and creator and not merely a doer of odd jobs which she is likely to become if she tries every type of work performed in the dean's office.

Intensive Inquiry of Questionnaire IV

The answers to certain questions asked in Questionnaire IV (see Appendix, p. 147) indicate the number of deans performing the specific types of work (see Table XXXI) which through interviews the writer found most general.

TABLE XXXI

DUTIES PERFORMED BY DEANS AND THEIR ASSISTANTS

DUTIES	BY WHOM PERFORMED *	Coed.		W.I.		W.A.		Total of All Colleges	
		No.	Per Cent	No.	Per Cent	No.	Per Cent	No.	Per Cent
SOCIAL DUTIES									
1. Work intimately with student government	(a)	66	78.6	13	76.5	6	100	85	79.4
	(b)	11		1		–		12	
	(c)	12		–		–		12	
	(d)	38		7		1		46	
	(e)	3		2		–		5	
2. Advise with Panhellenic	(a)	57	67.9	1	5.9	1	16.7	59	55.1
	(b)	9		–		–		9	
	(c)	9		–		–		9	
	(d)	3		–		–		3	
	(e)	2		–		–		2	
3. Supervise in general extra-curricular activities	(a)	64	76.2	13	76.5	4	66.7	81	75.7
	(b)	10		1		2		13	
	(c)	10		1		1		12	
	(d)	29		–		–		29	
	(e)	4		–		–		4	
4. Supervise social calendar	(a)	56	66.7	12	70.6	5	83.3	73	68.2
	(b)	10		–		1		11	
	(c)	6		–		–		6	
	(d)	11		1		–		12	
	(e)	4		–		1		5	
5. Approve chaperons for parties	(a)	63	75.0	9	52.9	3	50.0	75	70.1
	(b)	11		3		1		15	
	(c)	5		2		–		7	
	(d)	3		–		–		3	
	(e)	3		2		–		5	
6. Personally chaperon parties	(a)	48	57.1	6	35.3	3	50.0	57	53.3
	(b)	11		4		1		16	
	(c)	3		1		–		4	
	(d)	4		–		–		4	
	(e)	4		2		–		6	

*(a) =Performed by dean.
(b) =Performed by dean's assistants.
(c) =Performed by dean and assistants.
(d) =Among duties taking most of dean's time.
(e) =Among duties taking most of assistants' time.

TABLE XXXI (*Continued*)

Duties	By Whom Performed	Coed.		W. I.		W. A.		Total of All Colleges	
		No.	Per Cent	No.	Per Cent	No.	Per Cent	No.	Per Cent
7. Have charge of discipline in regard to nonacademic matters ..	(a)	69	82.1	12	70.6	6	100	87	81.3
	(b)	3		1		–		4	
	(c)	1		–		–		1	
	(d)	12		3		–		15	
	(e)	1		–		–		1	
8. Interview students in regard to their individual problems, i.e., do personnel work .	(a)	70	83.3	16	94.1	4	66.7	90	84.1
	(b)	14		1		1		16	
	(c)	13		1		1		15	
	(d)	54		10		2		66	
	(e)	4		1		–		5	
9. Entertain many college visitors ..	(a)	48	57.1	9	52.9	4	66.7	61	57.0
	(b)	5		1		1		7	
	(c)	2		1		–		3	
	(d)	–		1		1		2	
	(e)	–		–		–		0	
10. Entertain many college students .	(a)	45	53.6	10	58.8	4	66.4	59	55.1
	(b)	5		–		1		6	
	(c)	2		–		–		2	
	(d)	–		1		1		2	
	(e)	–		–		–		0	
ACADEMIC DUTIES									
11. Determine admissions	(a)	23	27.4	6	35.3	3	50.0	32	29.9
	(b)	–		1		2		3	
	(c)	–		–		–		0	
	(d)	2		–		1		3	
	(e)	–		1		1		2	
12. Have chief responsibility in regard to entrance examinations ...	(a)	–	–	3	17.6	1	16.7	4	3.7
	(b)	–		–		1		1	
	(c)	–		–		–		0	
	(d)	–		–		–		0	
	(e)	–		–		1		1	

TABLE XXXI (*Continued*)

Duties	By Whom Performed	Coed.		W.I.		W.A.		Total of All Colleges	
		No.	Per Cent	No.	Per Cent	No.	Per Cent	No.	Per Cent
13. Guide policy in regard to curriculum	(a)	13	15.5	7	41.2	6	100.	26	24.3
	(b)	—		—		–		0	
	(c)	—		—		–		0	
	(d)	4		1		1		6	
	(e)	—		—		–		0	
14. Supervise catalogue	(a)	2	2.4	8	47.1	2	33.3	12	11.2
	(b)	—		—		2		2	
	(c)	—		—		–		0	
	(d)	—		1		–		1	
	(e)	—		—		–		0	
15. Make academic adjustment for students who fail	(a)	46	54.8	11	64.7	5	83.3	62	57.9
	(b)	1		—		1		2	
	(c)	2		—		–		2	
	(d)	6		2		–		8	
	(e)	1		—		–		1	
16. Have interviews with students on academic questions	(a)	60	71.4	15	88.2	5	83.3	80	74.8
	(b)	3		—		1		4	
	(c)	4		—		–		4	
	(d)	18		12		3		33	
	(e)	—		—		–		0	
17. Administer student loans	(a)	41	48.8	4	23.5	3	50.0	48	44.9
	(b)	1		—		–		0	
	(c)	—		—		–		0	
	(d)	1		1		–		2	
	(e)	—		—		–		0	
18. Administer scholarship funds ...	(a)	37	44.0	6	35.3	4	66.7	47	43.9
	(b)	1		—		–		1	
	(c)	—		—		–		0	
	(d)	1		—		–		1	
	(e)	—		—		–		0	

TABLE XXXI (*Continued*)

DUTIES	BY WHOM PER- FORMED	FREQUENCY							
		Coed.		W. I.		W. A.		Total of All Colleges	
		No.	Per Cent	No.	Per Cent	No.	Per Cent	No.	Per Cent
19. Have responsibility for discipline on academic matters	(a)	42	50.0	13	76.5	5	83.3	60	56.1
	(b)	—		—		–		0	
	(c)	—		—		–		0	
	(d)	2		1		1		4	
	(e)	—		—		–		0	
20. Give excuses for absence	(a)	39	46.4	7	41.2	1	16.7	47	43.9
	(b)	7		—		3		10	
	(c)	5		—		–		5	
	(d)	3		1		–		4	
	(e)	4		—		2		6	
DUTIES IN CONNEC- TION WITH HEALTH									
21. Supervise food provided by college	(a)	10	11.9	—	—	1	16.7	11	10.3
	(b)	12		5		3		20	
	(c)	1		—		–		1	
	(d)	2		—		–		2	
	(e)	8		3		1		12	
22. Supervise house- keeping	(a)	13	15.4	0	—	1		14	13.0
	(b)	31							
	(c)	1							
	(d)	3							
	(e)	17							
23. Supervise infirm- ary	(a)	15	17.9	5	29.4	1	16.7	21	19.6
	(b)	4		—		–		4	
	(c)	1		—		–		1	
	(d)	—		—		–		0	
	(e)	1		—		–		1	
24. Initiate health projects	(a)	23	27.4	5	29.4	1	16.7	29	27.1
	(b)	4		—		–		4	
	(c)	1		—		–		1	
	(d)	—		—		–		0	
	(e)	—		—		–		0	

TABLE XXXI (*Continued*)

DUTIES	BY WHOM PER-FORMED	Coed.		W. I.		W. A.		Total of All Colleges	
		No.	Per Cent	No.	Per Cent	No.	Per Cent	No.	Per Cent
25. Give talks on health	(a)	13	15.5	4	23.5	3	50.0	20	18.7
	(b)	3		—		—		3	
	(c)	1		—		—		1	
	(d)	—		—		—		0	
	(e)	—		—		—		0	
26. Secure speakers on health	(a)	30	35.7	3	17.6	—	—	33	30.8
	(b)	4		1		—		5	
	(c)	1		—		—		1	
	(d)	3		—		—		3	
	(e)	4		1		—		5	
27. Inspect and approve off-campus lodging houses ..	(a)	42	50.0	1	5.9	1	16.7	44	41.1
	(b)	10		1		1		12	
	(c)	5		—		—		5	
	(d)	4		1		—		5	
	(e)	2		—		1		3	
DUTIES CONNECTED WITH VOCATIONAL GUIDANCE									
28. Give vocational information	(a)	54	64.3	9	52.9	2	33.3	65	60.7
	(b)	3		2		2		7	
	(c)	2		—		—		2	
	(d)	—		—		—		0	
	(e)	1		2		1		4	
29. Secure persons who give vocational guidance..	(a)	43	51.2	7	41.2	2	33.3	52	48.6
	(b)	2		2		2		6	
	(c)	1		—		—		1	
	(d)	2		—		—		2	
	(e)	—		1		1		2	
30. Systematically advise students in regard to vocations	(a)	28	33.3	7	41.2	1	16.7	36	33.6
	(b)	3		2		3		8	
	(c)	1		—		—		1	
	(d)	3		—		—		3	
	(e)	5		2		1		8	

TABLE XXXI (*Continued*)

DUTIES	BY WHOM PER-FORMED	Coed.		W. I.		W. A.		Total of All Colleges	
		No.	Per Cent	No.	Per Cent	No.	Per Cent	No.	Per Cent
31. Have charge of part-time employment	(a)	39	46.4	5	29.4	3	50.0	47	43.9
	(b)	6		1		3		10	
	(c)	2		—		–		2	
	(d)	1		1		–		2	
	(e)	1		1		–		2	
32. Have charge of permanent employment	(a)	20	23.8	2	11.8	1	16.7	23	21.5
	(b)	4		1		1		6	
	(c)	2		—		–		2	
	(d)	—		—		1		1	
	(e)	—		1		–		1	
ADMINISTRATIVE DUTIES									
33. Select members of the college staff like the registrar, etc.	(a)	7	8.3	—	—	2	33.3	9	8.4
	(b)	—		—		–		0	
	(c)	—		—		–		0	
	(d)	—		—		–		0	
	(e)	—		—		–		0	
34. Approve selection of college staff ..	(a)	12	14.3	2	11.8	4	66.7	18	16.8
	(b)	—		—		–		0	
	(c)	—		—		–		0	
	(d)	—		—		–		0	
	(e)	—		—		–		0	
35. Selection of members of faculty ..	(a)	10	11.9	—	—	1	16.7	11	10.5
	(b)	—		—		–		0	
	(c)	—		—		–		0	
	(d)	—		—		–		0	
	(e)	—		—		–		0	
36. Approve selection of members of faculty	(a)	11	13.1	3	17.6	5	83.3	19	17.8
	(b)	—		—		–		0	
	(c)	—		—		–		0	
	(d)	1		—		–		1	
	(e)	—		—		–		0	

TABLE XXXI (*Continued*)

DUTIES	BY WHOM PER-FORMED	FREQUENCY							
		Coed.		W. I.		W. A.		Total of All Colleges	
		No.	Per Cent	No.	Per Cent	No.	Per Cent	No.	Per Cent
37. Conduct faculty meetings	(a)	2	2.4	6	35.3	2	33.3	10	9.3
	(b)	—		—		–		0	
	(c)	—		—		–		0	
	(d)	—		—		–		0	
	(e)	—		—		–		0	
38. Approve plans for dormitories for women	(a)	55	65.5	5	29.4	5	83.3	65	60.7
	(b)	2		—		–		2	
	(c)	—		—		–		0	
	(d)	—		—		–		0	
	(e)	—		—		–		0	
39. Approve plans for other college buildings	(a)	9	10.7	2	11.8	5	83.3	16	15.0
	(b)	—		—		–		0	
	(c)	—		—		–		0	
	(d)	1		—		–		1	
	(e)	—		—		–		0	
40. Approve purchase of equipment for dormitories for women	(a)	52	61.9	6	35.3	5	83.3	63	58.9
	(b)	2		—		1		3	
	(c)	3		—		1		3	
	(d)	1		—		–		1	
	(e)	—		—		–		0	
41. Approve purchase of equipment for other buildings .	(a)	8	9.5	1	5.9	2	33.3	11	10.3
	(b)	1		—		1		2	
	(c)	—		—		–		0	
	(d)	—		—		–		0	
	(e)	—		—		–		0	
42. Meet regularly with trustees of college	(a)	7	8.3	3	17.6	3	16.7	11	10.3
	(b)	—		—		–		0	
	(c)	—		—		–		0	
	(d)	1		—		1		2	
	(e)	—		—		–		0	

TABLE XXXI (*Continued*)

Duties	By Whom Per-formed	Coed.		W. I.		W. A.		Total of All Colleges	
		No.	Per Cent	No.	Per Cent	No.	Per Cent	No.	Per Cent
43. Interview the faculty educational policies	(a)	24	28.6	11	64.7	6	100	41	38.3
	(b)	—		—		–		0	
	(c)	—		—		–		0	
	(d)	3		3		1		7	
	(e)	—		—		–		0	
44. Raise money for the college	(a)	12	14.3	2	11.8	2	33.3	10	15.0
	(b)	—		—		–		0	
	(c)	1		—		–		1	
	(d)	1		—		2		3	
	(e)	—		—		–		0	
45. Plan chapel exercises	(a)	11	13.1	8	47.1	1	16.7	20	18.7
	(b)	1		—		–		1	
	(c)	—		—		–		0	
	(d)	1		—		1		2	
	(e)	—		—		–		0	
46. Regularly lead chapel exercises .	(a)	18	21.4	11	64.7	3	50.0	32	29.9
	(b)	1		—		–		1	
	(c)	—		—		–		0	
	(d)	1		—		–		1	
	(e)	—		—		–		0	
47. Regularly attend chapel	(a)	42	51.2	12	70.6	3	50.0	58	54.2
	(b)	1		1		–		2	
	(c)	1		—		–		1	
	(d)	1		—		–		1	
	(e)	—		—		–		0	
48. Supervise the religious activities .	(a)	38	45.2	7	41.2	1	16.7	46	43.0
	(b)	1		—		–		1	
	(c)	—		—		–		0	
	(d)	—		—		–		0	
	(e)	—		—		–		0	

TABLE XXXI (*Continued*)

DUTIES	BY WHOM PER-FORMED	FREQUENCY							
		Coed.		W. I.		W. A.		Total of All Colleges	
		No.	Per Cent	No.	Per Cent	No.	Per Cent	No.	Per Cent
49. Secure speakers on religious subjects	(a)	20	23.8	5	29.4	1	16.7	26	24.3
	(b)	1		—		–		1	
	(c)	1		—		–		1	
	(d)	—		1		–		1	
	(e)	—		—		–		0	

SOCIAL DUTIES OF THE DEAN

Student Government. In name at least, student government has pervaded the American institutions of higher learning. The organization and methods of procedure, it is true, vary in different colleges and universities. In some the students have nominally the power to regulate their own conduct, but actually the power is in the hands of the faculty; the student government officers merely serve as a connecting link between faculty and students. In other institutions, every effort is made to have students make their own regulations and enforce them. In the majority of institutions, faculty and students work together, and the dean is the person who most frequently serves in an advisory capacity to women students. We note the high percentage of deans working with student government in each of the three types of institutions:

66, or 79 per cent, of the coeducational institutions
13, or 77 per cent, of the independent colleges for women
6, or 100 per cent, of the affiliated colleges
85, or 79 per cent, of all institutions

Panhellenic. The Panhellenic Association on a college campus is an organization composed of representatives from the Greek-letter societies. In many institutions it is an organization of power which can aid greatly in furthering high standards of scholarship and conduct on the campus. Work with the central organization

entails, as well, advisory work with the individual sororities.   In
colleges for women sororities are rarely found; therefore we find
the deans' work with the sororities in

57, or 68 per cent, of the coeducational institutions
1, or 6 per cent, of the independent colleges for women
1, or 17 per cent, of the affiliated colleges for women
59, or 55 per cent, of all institutions

Extra-Curricular Activities. The extra-curricular activities are
those organized student enterprises, clubs, celebrations, projects,
and the like, which nominally do not have a place in the course of
study but which play an important part in modern education.   In
a sense, student government and Panhellenic are in this category,
but they were considered units of work by themselves by so many
deans that they were given places by themselves in the investigation.   Extra-curricular activities, in general, are supervised by
deans in

64, or 76 per cent, of the coeducational institutions
13, or 77 per cent, of the independent colleges for women
4, or 67 per cent, of the affiliated colleges for women
81, or 76 per cent, of all institutions.

Social Calendar. The supervision of the social calendar usually
entails approval of the nature and number of social functions
attended by women, the arrangement as to dates, and the issuing
of the weekly calendar of events.   To this duty deans lay claim in

56, or 67 per cent, of the coeducational institutions
12, or 71 per cent, of the independent colleges for women
5, or 83 per cent, of the affiliated colleges for women
73, or 68 per cent, of all institutions

Chaperonage. It is a regulation in most colleges and universities
that social functions attended by women students must be chaper-
oned by persons approved by the college authorities.   In some
institutions the chaperons are given definite instructions concerning
their duties and asked to file a report at the dean's office after the
party.   Approval of chaperons is given by deans in

63, or 75 per cent, of the coeducational institutions
9, or 53 per cent, of the independent colleges for women
3, or 50 per cent, of the affiliated colleges for women
75, or 70 per cent, of all institutions

Personal Chaperonage of Parties. Nearly all deans are obliged to attend many social functions. The importance of the dean's position in the institution necessitates her presence at formal functions and her personal relationship to students occasions her attendance at many informal affairs. The tendency of the dean to act in person as a chaperon appears to be on the wane. The writer did not find one dean in a Grade A college who is expected personally to chaperon every social function attended by women and to stay until the end of each party. In general, however, deans attend a great many functions and chaperon comparatively few. The deans in coeducational colleges for women chaperon least. The figures show that deans sometimes act personally as chaperons in

48, or 57 per cent, of the coeducational institutions
6, or 35 per cent, of the independent colleges for women
3, or 50 per cent, of the affiliated colleges
57, or 53 per cent, of all institutions

Discipline in Nonacademic Matters. Owing to the prevalence of student government in American colleges and universities, some deans queried found it difficult to answer in regard to their responsibility concerning discipline in nonacademic matters. There were some who disclaimed responsibility for the discipline though they spent a large part of their time in working with student government. Some replied that ordinary cases were taken care of by student government but that certain types of offenses came only to the dean or to the dean and the president. In general, the deans felt that if "having charge of discipline" means being in the last analysis responsible for the conduct of women students, then they were in charge. The answers indicated that in respect to discipline, constructive and preventive work is fast superseding the old system of rules and penalties. Responsibility for discipline in regard to nonacademic matters is claimed by deans in

69, or 82 per cent, of the coeducational institutions
12, or 71 per cent, of the independent colleges for women
6, or 100 per cent, of the affiliated colleges
87, or 81 per cent, of all institutions

Personnel Work. It is essential that students have some person with whom they can advise concerning their individual problems. Different institutions have various ways of meeting the need. A rather common device has been the distribution of students in groups of fifteen or fifty among the members of the faculty, each of whom is expected to act as adviser to the students in his group, on any matter related to their welfare. Sometimes this plan has worked out well; often it has proved unsatisfactory because the faculty advisers were too busy to give the student adequate attention or not skillful in winning their confidence. Increasingly in colleges there is a tendency to put the advisory work in the hands of a few highly skilled persons chosen for that work. Northwestern University has a personnel department with a director which coördinates all efforts in student guidance in that institution. Smith College has recently centralized its personnel under one officer. The amount of personnel work that the dean does will depend, of course, on what other provision is made for it, her liking for the work and skill in it, and the amount of time she can spare for other duties. In many institutions all the systematic personnel work done for women students is in the hands of the dean. This duty, it should be noted, is performed by more deans than any other. The figures are:

70, or 83 per cent, in the coeducational institutions
16, or 94 per cent, in the independent colleges for women
4, or 67 per cent, in the affiliated colleges for women
90, or 84 per cent, in all institutions

Entertainment of College Visitors. It has been mentioned in connection with salary that the woman dean frequently does a great deal of entertaining. In some institutions it is understood that she will act as official hostess to distinguished personages, visiting organizations, and groups of alumnae. Frequently the matter of entertainment is left to her own discretion. The deans who entertain many visitors are:

48, or 57 per cent, in the coeducational institutions
9, or 53 per cent, in the independent colleges for women
4, or 67 per cent, in the affiliated colleges
61, or 57 per cent, in all institutions

Entertainment of College Students. One dean in a large state university told the writer that during one university year she entertained in her own home tweny-five hundred students. The deans who entertain many students, the writer noticed, are in general the same deans who entertain many visitors. There were:

45, or 54 per cent, in the coeducational institutions
10, or 59 per cent, in the colleges for women
4, or 67 per cent, in the affiliated colleges
59, or 55 per cent, in all institutions

Summary for Social Duties. Social duties appear to be very general for deans, regardless of the type of deanship. No one of the ten duties enumerated, however, is performed by every dean. The duties which are most generally performed by deans in all types of institutions are concerned with student government of the institutions, extra-curricular activities, and personnel work. Deans in coeducational institutions more than those in the other types, must work with sororities; they are more frequently concerned with chaperonage in the way of approving chaperons and actually chaperoning in person. In general, it may be concluded, all deans have many social duties, and there do not appear to be great differences in the nature of such duties which are due to the different types of organization. Such differences as exist are related apparently to the quantity rather than the kind of social duties.

ACADEMIC DUTIES

From the interviews with deans, it was found that there were ten academic duties most commonly performed.

Admissions. The determining of admissions is one. The increasing number of women students now attending college has made the problem of who shall be admitted of great significance. Privately endowed institutions in particular are setting up for admission not only higher barriers in scholarship, but other standards in regard to personality. Even state institutions, which aim to be as democratic as possible, are tightening entrance requirements. Deans in coeducational institutions who concern themselves with admissions do so often by virtue of membership on a committee dealing with admissions or they are asked by the president of a committee in doubtful cases to pass on the eligibility of certain women students. In a few cases they have personal interviews with applicants for admission. With the academic aspect of admissions, these deans appear very little concerned. Deans have some concern with admissions in

23, or 27 per cent, of the coeducational institutions
6, or 35 per cent, of the independent colleges for women

3, or 50 per cent, of the affiliated colleges
32, or 30 per cent, of all institutions

Entrance Examinations. No dean in a coeducational institution has responsibility for entrance examinations; three deans in the independent colleges have; and one in the affiliated has.

Policy in Regard to Curriculum. Deans in coeducational colleges, if one can judge from their comments, would like to have opportunity to influence the policies of curriculum in the interests of women students to a greater extent than is usually allowed. There is spreading among educators the conviction that the modern college curriculum should provide sex differentiation in education. Until recent years women have been content with the opportunity of demonstrating that they could pass with credit the same courses that men take. Now they are asking for special work to fit their special needs. Colleges for women are aiming to meet the need; Vassar has its course in euthenics; Smith, its experiment in the coördination of women's interests. In coeducational institutions, men professors aim to further the interests of women students but are often not in sufficiently close touch with them to understand their needs. A dean of women who has vision and is given an opportunity to present the needs of women does a great deal to keep the institution educationally abreast of the times. In 84 per cent of the coeducational institutions noted, the dean can have only an indirect influence on such policies. Deans who can directly shape policies in regard to curriculum are:

13, or 16 per cent, in coeducational institutions
7, or 41 per cent, in independent colleges for women
6, or 100 per cent, in affiliated colleges
26, or 24 per cent, in all institutions

Supervision of the Catalogue. More deans in independent colleges for women supervise the catalogue than in coeducational or affiliated institutions. The figures are:

2, or 2 per cent, in coeducational institutions
8, or 47 per cent, in independent colleges for women
2, or 33 per cent, in affiliated colleges
12, or 11 per cent, in all institutions

Adjustment of Academic Failures. The replies from deans in regard to this item indicate that they are all concerned with women students who fail in studies. A few explained that they sit on faculty committees which dealt with all failures; others, all in coeducational institutions, said that they always tried to discover the cause of a girl's failure and to take remedial measures but they had no power to make a readjustment for her from an academic point of view. They could investigate and make some provision for her health, social activities, and finances, but in regard to her studies they could only advise unofficially. In only one coeducational institution did the investigator find that the course of study of every girl must have final approval from the office of the dean of women. The deans in the other two types of institution more frequently advise concerning courses of study and make an academic adjustment for students who fail. Some sort of adjustment is made by

46, or 55 per cent, in coeducational institutions
11, or 65 per cent, in independent colleges for women
 5, or 83 per cent, in affiliated colleges
62, or 58 per cent, in all institutions

Interviews on Academic Matters. To this question we find a larger number of deans in coeducational institutions answering affirmatively than to the preceding one. Naturally in the course of their personnel work they will be consulted in regard to a great many academic problems which officially they can not settle. They can give the student helpful advice; they can sometimes present the student's problem to the faculty. Certainly, if they are to be effective deans, they must work in the closest coöperation with the persons who officially handle academic problems. In colleges for women the interview on academic matters is one of the deans' most important duties.

Interviews are held by

60, or 71 per cent, in coeducational institutions
15, or 88 per cent, in independent colleges for women
 5, or 83 per cent, in affiliated colleges
80, or 75 per cent, in all institutions

Administration of Student Loans. Frequently the decisions in regard to student loans are in the hands of the faculty committee. Often in a coeducational institution the dean is a member of that committee. Whether she is or not, the tendency is apparently to take her recommendation as final in regard to women students. Deans have the administration of such loans in

   41, or 49 per cent, of the coeducational institutions
   4, or 24 per cent, of the women's independent colleges
   3, or 50 per cent, of the affiliated colleges
   48, or 45 per cent, of all institutions

Administration of Scholarship Funds. Not so many deans in coeducational institutions administer scholarship funds as administer loans to women, the reason being that other members of the faculty are particularly interested in matters pertaining to scholarship. On the other hand, more deans in colleges for women perform this duty than administer loans. The figures are:

   37, or 44 per cent, in coeducational institutions
   6, or 35 per cent, in independent colleges for women
   4, or 67 per cent, in affiliated colleges
   47, or 44 per cent, in all institutions

Discipline on Academic Matters. In regard to this duty, the replies of deans in interviews and their responses to Questionnaire III show a sharp differentiation in the three types of institution. The dean in the coeducational institution in which she has anything to do with discipline on academic matters is usually concerned with it by virtue of her position on a faculty committee serving for both men and women or she may advise officially or unofficially a student government committee dealing with cases of cheating. The dean of the independent college for women has more responsibility and more authority. She may be chairman of a committee on academic matters or she may have the recommendation of a committee referred to her for a decision. In an important matter she makes a decision after consultation with the president. The dean in an affiliated college is usually the final authority in a given case. The figures are:

   42, or 50 per cent, in coeducational institutions
   13, or 77 per cent, in independent colleges for women
   5, or 83 per cent, in affiliated colleges
   60, or 56 per cent, in all institutions

Excuses for Absence. In the early days of the woman dean the giving of permission and excuses was an important duty. Nowadays it is less often their task. For one reason, in regard to

absence from class, fewer excuses are demanded, the modern tendency being to let the absentee from a class make such adjustment
with the instructor as she can.   Again, in institutions where excuses are still given, deans of every type are more and more being
relieved of clerical work that they may have more time for the
big movements on the college campus.   Permissions to leave town
are usually obtained by girls living in college dormitories from the
heads of the halls. The duty of granting permissions and excuses
is performed by deans in

  39, or 46 per cent, of the coeducational institutions
  7, or 41 per cent, of the independent colleges for women
  1, or 17 per cent, of the affiliated colleges
  47, or 44 per cent, of all institutions

Summary of Academic Duties.   No dean in a coeducational institution has the chief responsibility in regard to entrance examinations.   The deans in colleges for women have more to do with
guiding policies of curriculum, supervising the catalogue, adjustments for students failing in studies, interviews with students on
academic matters, and discipline in all academic matters.   Even
without a quantitative measure of the amount of work done, the
difference between the type of work done by deans in coeducational institutions and that done by deans in colleges for women
is more pronounced than it was with reference to social duties.
Comparing the figures for the two types of deans in colleges for
women, we find a tendency toward more authority in the hands
of the dean in the affiliated college.

DUTIES IN CONNECTION WITH HEALTH

Every type of dean is perforce interested in health. If her duties
are chiefly social, she is interested in health with reference to
extra-curricular activities. If she spends much time in personnel
work, the question of physical and mental health is to be considered if not thoroughly investigated. If her duties are chiefly
academic, she must study the effect of health on scholarship. If
she is chiefly an administrator of the entire college, she must have
the health of students in mind in almost every decision she makes.
When the returns from Questionnaire IV were received, the
writer was convinced that deans spend much more time in working for the interests of good health than the answers numbered

21 to 27 seem to indicate. Interview and correspondence deep-
ened this conviction. Many institutions have well-established
health departments with competent persons in charge. A dean, in
consequence, is reluctant to assume credit for initiating health
projects, giving talks on health, or securing speakers who give such
talks. Even the dean of an affiliated college feels, however frequently she may give suggestions to the department of health, that
theirs is the responsibility for health, and theirs should be the
credit.

In the eyes of some college presidents the dean has more responsibility than she is willing to claim. For example, the writer compared the answers given by some deans in coeducational colleges in
regard to supervision of food with answers on the same point sent
in by the presidents of the same institutions in response to a questionnaire sent out by a student of research in housing. It was
found in a number of instances that the dean in this investigation
disclaimed responsibility for food, whereas the president informed
the investigator that it was the dean's. The dean, it is easy to conclude, has so little first-hand supervision of the food that she did
not feel the responsibility. Trained dietitians made it unnecessary
for her to do so. The president, casting around in his mind, as he
answers his questionnaire, for the person whom, after him, he
would hold responsible for the food of women students, decides
it is the dean and answers accordingly.

Inspection and Approval of Lodgings. One task which an ap-
preciable number of deans perform is the inspection and approval
of off-campus lodgings. This responsibility comes from the belief
that education through environment is as important as education
from books, and that if institutions can not provide living quarters
and food for their students in college buildings they must at least
see to it that suitable quarters are provided elsewhere.

The duty is performed chiefly by deans in coeducational institutions. Colleges for women are more likely to have most of their
students on the campus. Mt. Holyoke at present has only four
students off-campus. Frequently in colleges for women, the matter
of housing is in the hands of a head or dean of residence, who
coöperates with the dean who is being considered in this study.

In some cases the inspection is perfunctory and a house once
approved and put on a registered list goes uninspected for years.
In other institutions each house is inspected annually and is given

a score according to a scale scientifically worked out. Landladies are organized and have frequent meetings for the purpose of finding solutions to common problems. A "Handbook for Landladies" is sometimes published by such an organization, food demonstrations are held, and a scale of prices for room and board fixed by common agreement. Usually the inception of such an organization is due to the dean or one of her staff and its success depends upon her leadership. The number of deans performing the duty is:

42, or 50 per cent, in coeducational institutions
1, or 6 per cent, in independent colleges for women
1, or 17 per cent, in affiliated colleges
44, or 41 per cent, in all institutions

Summary of Duties in Connection with Health. Deans, it appears, are more concerned with problems of health than is indicated by the answers to Questionnaire III. Direct responsibility in regard to food, housekeeping, infirmary, health projects and off-campus lodgings is claimed by only one dean in an affiliated college. Three deans in the group give talks on health.

In the independent colleges for women no dean looks after food or housekeeping. The number directly responsible for other duties in connection with health is small.

Deans in coeducational institutions are more directly concerned with the health of women students and the duty most often claiming their attention is the inspection and approval of off-campus houses. All the deans, it should be noted, who do personnel work, are constantly dealing with problems of physical and mental health.

VOCATIONAL GUIDANCE

Within recent years institutions have begun to take cognizance of their responsibility for the vocational guidance of students. Even those colleges which have withstood the demand for vocational education, aiming at a purely cultural course, have attempted vocational guidance. Of the several services included in vocational guidance by the dean, probably the most frequently rendered is the dissemination of information about vocations. College women are eagerly inquiring concerning the occupational opportunities open to them. Many deans try to answer their questions by arranging more or less formal opportunity for them to find out the necessary facts.

From the replies to Questionnaire III we note that a large percentage of all deans give vocational information. In amount such information varies from the occasional answer to the questions of the students to a carefully worked out series of talks and even interviews with every student. Affirmative answers to this question came from

54, or 64 per cent of deans, in coeducational institutions
9, or 53 per cent of deans, in independent colleges for women
2, or 33 per cent, in affiliated colleges
65, or 61 per cent, in all institutions

Securing Speakers. Deans frequently secure outside speakers to give vocational information to women students. Sometimes they organize a "Vocational Week" in which representatives from various vocations open to women visit the college campus, lecture and hold clinics. Again, the information is distributed through the year by experts in the field of vocational guidance such as the representatives from the Bureau of Vocational Information. Deans securing speakers number

43, or 51 per cent, in coeducational institutions
7, or 41 per cent, in independent colleges for women
2, or 33 per cent, in affiliated colleges for women
52, or 49 per cent, of all institutions

Systematic Advising of Students. Too often in the past vocational advice was not given to students until they were about to leave an institution. The inadequacy of such procedure is now apparent and an effort is made to give information and advice early in the student's college career. Sometimes in coeducational institutions the dean gives a course in vocations required of all freshman women. Deans who reported that they give systematic advice are:

28, or 33 per cent, in coeducational institutions
7, or 41 per cent, in independent colleges for women
1, or 17 per cent, in affiliated colleges for women
36, or 34 per cent, in all institutions

In view, however, of the admittedly immature development of vocational guidance in colleges, it is hardly likely that this work which is reported as "systematic" is more than rudimentary.

Direction of Part-Time Employment. Europeans are astounded by the number of women students in America who work their way wholly or in part through college. For example, three hundred freshman women who had to find work if they stayed in the university came to Cornell University in 1926. It is often possible for American students to work and study at the same time because the dean assists them in finding suitable employment and supervises closely their health, studies, and social life while they work. At the University of Indiana, for one, the work of part-time employment is most efficiently managed by the dean's office. The dean has this responsibility in

39, or 46 per cent, of the coeducational institutions
5, or 29 per cent, of the independent colleges for women
3, or 50 per cent, of the affiliated colleges for women
47, or 44 per cent of all institutions

Direction of Permanent Employment. By permanent employment, deans sometimes mean full-time positions, as distinguished from part-time positions held by students while they are attending college; for example, a position as stenographer held during the day by a young woman who attends classes in a municipal university in the evening. Often, however, the term refers to the employment of students after leaving college.

Because the dean has supposedly the opportunity to know many students personally, she has in some colleges been put in charge of the placement of women graduates. Deans in charge of permanent employment are:

20, or 24 per cent, in coeducational institutions
5, or 29 per cent, in independent colleges for women
1, or 17 per cent, in affiliated colleges for women
23, or 22 per cent, in all institutions

Summary of Duties in Vocational Guidance. The figures given indicate an active interest in vocational guidance on the part of deans in each type of institution. Deans in coeducational institutions and in independent colleges for women appear to have rather more intimate contact with it. The two phases of vocational guidance with which they are most commonly occupied are the disseminating of vocational information and the management of part-time employment.

ADMINISTRATIVE DUTIES

The answers regarding only six of the administrative duties included in the questionnaire appear to be worthy of detailed statement.

Approval of the Selection of College Staff. This duty is performed by deans in

    12, or 14 per cent, of the coeducational institutions
    2, or 12 per cent, of the independent colleges for women
    4, or 67 per cent, of the affiliated colleges
    18, or 17 per cent, of all institutions

Approval of Selection of Members of the Faculty. Inquiry subsequent to the receipt of the answers showed that those deans in coeducational institutions who claimed to approve selection of the members of the faculty usually referred to members of their own staffs or to the approval they give unofficially to the president when he advises with them. In the allied colleges, only one dean actually selects the faculty but five feel that they have a deciding vote. The figures are:

    11, or 13 per cent, in coeducational institutions
    3, or 18 per cent, in independent colleges for women
    5, or 83 per cent, in affiliated colleges
    19, or 18 per cent, in all institutions.

Approval of Plans for Dormitories for Women. This duty is least often performed by deans in independent colleges. We might suppose a sufficient reason to be that plans for dormitories are looked after by the dean of residence if we did not find that only two deans in these colleges approve plans of other buildings. The figures concerning dormitories are:

    55, or 66 per cent, in coeducational institutions
    5, or 29 per cent, in independent colleges for women
    5, or 83 per cent, in affiliated colleges
    65, or 61 per cent, in all institutions

Approval of Plans for Other College Buildings. This is given by deans in

    9, or 11 per cent, of coeducational institutions
    2, or 12 per cent, of independent colleges for women
    5, or 83 per cent, of affiliated colleges
    16, or 15 per cent, of all institutions

Approval of Purchase of Equipment for Dormitories for Women. This is given by deans in

52, or 62 per cent, of coeducational institutions
6, or 35 per cent, of independent colleges
5, or 83 per cent, of affiliated colleges
63, or 59 per cent, of all institutions

Interviewing Faculty on Educational Policies. In regard to this duty we find a striking differentiation. To interview the faculty is an important part of the work of the deans in the two types of colleges for women and is recognized as such by the president and the members of the faculty. In coeducational institutions the duty is less often performed by a dean, and when it is, the interview is less often a frontal attack on the problem. The dean must, the writer is told, secure coöperation for policies she advocates by the methods by which women were formerly supposed to influence politics. In some institutions the faculty would gladly be interviewed by the dean on any problem relative to the social life or housing, but would resent any initiative on her part in regard to academic matters. In many institutions the dean herself would not feel that academic policies were in her province. In a very few coeducational institutions she would have as active and as vital an interest in academic matters as the head of any department would. The figures for this duty are:

24, or 29 per cent, of the coeducational institutions
11, or 65 per cent, of the independent colleges for women
6, or 100 per cent, of affiliated colleges
41, or 38 per cent, of all institutions

Summary of Administrative Duties. Administrative duties are most numerous among deans of affiliated colleges, least among the deans in independent colleges for women. The deans in the affiliated colleges most frequently approve the selection of the faculty, approve plans for dormitories for women, approve plans for other college buildings; approve purchase for equipment for dormitories, and interview the faculty with reference to educational policies. With the exception of the last, deans in coeducational institutions are next in frequency in performing these duties. This, which is more academic in nature than the others, is performed by about two-thirds of the deans in independent colleges for women.

Duties Connected with Religion

The deans in the independent colleges for women, it appears, figure more prominently in the religious life of their institutions than do deans in other types of institutions. Forty-seven per cent of them plan chapel exercises, 65 per cent regularly lead chapel exercises; 71 per cent regularly attend chapel; 41 per cent supervise the religious activities on the campus; and 29 per cent secure speakers on religious subjects. Coeducational institutions, particularly universities, are less likely to have chapel exercises, and the religious activities are often in charge of a person specially trained and appointed for the work. Even so, 45 per cent of deans in coeducational institutions supervise the religious activities. The deans in affiliated colleges, with these duties as with many others, have less first-hand contact because the responsibility they carry in regard to the entire organization leaves them no time for it.

Other Duties

The duties discussed above do not form a complete picture of the work of deans. It is conceivable that deans who did not answer the questionnaire may not find in the previous discussion those duties performed by them which they consider most important. Or, deans who did answer may find that their most important duties are different from those of a year ago. Twenty-one duties in all were added to the list by the deans who answered. Several deans suggested that in a discussion of the duties, the investigator lay particular stress upon the dean's social activities, work for publicity for the institution, and personnel work. The five types of activity in which the dean engages, chiefly with reference to these kinds of work, are: interviews, speechmaking, attendance at social functions and meetings, research, and correspondence.

Interviews. Concerning the amount of time which they give to interviews, the deans could give only approximate answers. Without a time-study, they maintain, it is impossible to state the relative place of the interview in the day's work. Face-to-face and telephone conversations in their offices constitute only a part of the time given. In the offices of the institutions, in their homes, or in dormitories, wherever they go, they are constantly having interviews with the president and other members of the faculty, with their assistants, students, parents, landladies and college visitors. Among the deans of women the greatest number of interviews has to do with personnel work for the students.

Speechmaking. A duty which does not appear to rest conspicuously on deans in colleges for women but which is growing increasingly heavy for deans in universities is the making of addresses. On the campus the student group in a university is large and there are many organizations before which the dean should appear. Her speeches vary from a fifteen-minute informal talk at a basketball rally to a carefully prepared address of two hours before an alumnae conference. Off-campus the dean has, as it were, a large body of constituents, persons and organizations that feel they have a right to call upon her, that she is—particularly if the university be state-supported—a servant of the public. The dean, desiring to connect her institution with various worthy organizations and anxious to interpret to the public the work for women students, accepts many invitations to speak.

The 107 deans concerned in this investigation were asked to state approximately the number of speeches they made in a year. Seven made none, 9 did not answer, the range in number for the others is from 1 to 180. The few deans at the upper end of the scale knew exactly how many speeches they made, for each kept a card index. Often, they explained, the same speech was used many times during a year. A number had definitely limited themselves to two or three addresses a week. The deans in independent colleges for women spoke chiefly within their own institutions. Deans in allied institutions frequently spoke in the effort to raise money, and two deans in coeducational institutions were doing the same. One had raised a large endowment fund for the work of her own department. Another had been obliged to put an extra assistant into her office while she toured the country to raise money for a student union.

The answers, though only approximately accurate, can certainly be considered an indication that speaking in public is an important part of a dean's work, particularly in a coeducational institution.

Attendance at Social Functions and Meetings. Another activity related to the dean's work for publicity is attendance at social functions and meetings. The activity ranges from taking tea informally with the wife of the president to representing the dean's own institution at a formal function in another large university. Deans in coeducational institutions have the greatest variety; deans in affiliated institutions naturally represent the institution more frequently on formal occasions.

A great deal of work is done by all three types of deans for off-campus organizations. These are commonly the American Association of University Women, one or more college alumnae associations, the state and national deans associations, and other bodies like the League of Nations Union, League of Women Voters, and the English-Speaking Union. A dean will belong, because of her own special interests, to some organizations like the Modern Language Association or National Geographic Society. She works for many in order to form contacts for her own institution. She attends meetings of these organizations, has interviews, makes speeches, and sometimes does research for them.

Research. We find that deans in institutions with a very large attendance, e.g., the University of California, are doing research with the aim of promoting the welfare of students. They realize that when dealing with such large numbers of students, they can do constructive work of permanent value only by basing such work on data scientifically gathered. Hence we find certain deans conducting investigations concerning scholarships, activities, means of transportation, and housing.

Correspondence. The activity of writing many letters appears to be most common among deans of women in coeducational institutions and deans of affiliated colleges. Among deans of women in particular, the investigator found increasing demands for clerical assistance to meet the pressure connected with research studies, correspondence, and the keeping of records.

Records. Table XXXII indicates which of fourteen records are kept by the dean in her own office for every girl, which are kept for special students only, and which records that are kept for every girl are accessible in some other office of the institution.

From the table we see that the record, barring residence, most often kept by deans in coeducational institutions is that of college activities, and, next, that of home-history. Deans in colleges for women appear more concerned with academic records. In independent colleges 10 have scores on mental tests in their own offices; 7 have academic grades; 4 keep honors; and 7, scholarships.

Inquiry among the deans elicited the information that it is

often more necessary for the dean in a coeducational institution to have records in her own office because of the arrangement of offices. Often the dean of women has an office far removed from those files which contain official records.

TABLE XXXII

RECORDS

(107 Cases)

RECORD	COED.			W. I.			W. A.			TOTAL		
	*a	*b	*c	a	b	c	a	b	c	a	b	c
1. Information about Parents	44	6	22	5	–	10	2	–	2	51	6	34
2. Secondary School	12	3	60	5	–	10	3	–	3	20	3	73
3. College Residence	66	3	10	13	–	3	4	1	1	83	4	14
4. Score on Mental Tests ..	22	5	38	10	–	4	3	2	1	35	7	43
5. College Academic Grades	26	11	40	7	–	8	4	–	2	37	11	50
6. College Normal	21	6	41	8	–	7	4	–	2	33	6	50
7. Scholarships	20	5	44	6	–	8	7	–	2	33	5	54
8. Loans	22	5	40	6	–	7	3	–	3	31	5	50
9. College Health Record ..	14	5	43	3	1	11	2	–	3	19	6	57
10. Times Disciplined	34	6	12	8	1	4	2	1	1	44	8	17
11. College Activities	48	2	15	7	1	3	4	–	2	59	3	20
12. Vocational Interest	29	4	14	7	1	4	2	1	2	38	6	20
13. Employment during College	20	3	21	6	1	3	2	–	2	28	4	26
14. Employment after College	14	2	30	7	1	7	3	–	2	24	3	39

* a = Record for every girl in dean's office.
 b = Record for special cases in dean's office.
 c = Record for every girl accessible in some other office.

QUANTITATIVE STUDY OF DUTIES PERFORMED

In the effort to obtain even an approximate idea of the types of work which consume the largest part of the dean's time, the deans were asked to name the three duties listed in Table XXXI with which they were chiefly engaged. A few deans found it impossible to determine. Some could not limit themselves to three and named four or five. Those deans in largest institutions, it appeared, could tell best, the reason for this being that types of work were more definitely parceled out among them and their assistants.

Among 84 deans in coeducational institutions, personnel work was named 56 times; student government, 40; and extra-curricular activities, 29. Interviews in academic questions were named 12 times by the 16 deans in independent colleges. From the 6 deans in affiliated colleges, there was a variety of answers. Three named interviews on academic questions.

TYPES OF DEANS

The data discussed above seem to confirm the point already made that there are three types of deans to correspond to the three types of college organizations discussed. There are overlappings, it is true, from one college to another with reference to duties. Student government and personnel work are problems common to all. All types, we have seen, have many social duties. Yet in each type of college, certain duties are performed by a larger percentage than in others. Grouped together, these duties show that the dean's work in those institutions is predominantly of a certain type.

In the independent college for women, the dean is concerned with degrees, interviews on academic questions, and educational policies. In the affiliated college, she is virtually the president, with distinctly administrative duties, such as selecting or approving members of staff and faculty, approving plans for college buildings, and guiding educational policies. The dean in the coeducational institution is the type that is socially most active. It appears that the classification of deans which has been made roughly in the past, and not based on comprehensive investigation, is as accurate as any that can be made in the present development of this profession. That classification has been administrative, academic, and social.

It is the dean of women or "social dean" who appears to be undergoing the greatest change at the present time. As the enrollment in colleges has increased and the need for guidance has become more apparent, the work of the dean of women has been broadening. To the social duties she has always had, she appears to be adding academic and administrative duties. Food and housing she less often supervises personally, but she must be familiar with the best methods of house-management in order to coöperate with the experts in charge and to coördinate their work. Her burden of personnel work has increased tremendously. Demands made upon her time by the public are legion.

It is this diversity and multiplicity of great responsibilities for this type of dean, no doubt, that leads to the new experiments that are being tried in the organization of the work of the dean of women. In one institution, a women's council is organized with a chairman at the head. This council, which consists of seventeen women members of the faculty in the university, meets monthly. An executive committee, consisting of five council members, meets weekly. The council is as follows: Chairman of the council, director of physical culture for women, medical adviser for women, chairman of the inter-house council, social director, director of women's clubhouse, representative of women's commons staff, four women deans, three persons known as the "senior women of the faculty," and three persons appointed by the president.

In another institution the work is divided among three advisers and an assistant—one adviser acting as chairman. These advisers have no teaching duties.

In a third university, one person has been placed at the head of all the work formerly done by nine advisers. There is still an adviser in each of the nine colleges, but at the head is the dean of women who coördinates their work and teaches a professional course for deans.

It is possible that these experiments are the beginning of a trend toward a decentralization of responsibilities which in the past have fallen to the lot of the dean of women in coeducational institutions. To date, however, the consensus of opinion is that in an institution attended by both men and women, there should be a woman who views the interests and needs of women students as a whole and acts as a coördinator of all campus efforts to meet those needs.

CHAPTER XI

CHARTING THE DAY'S WORK OF THE DEAN OF WOMEN

TIME-STUDY OF THE DUTIES OF TWO DEANS

As a quantitative measure of the work performed by one type of dean, a time chart was kept for two weeks in the last term of the academic year by deans in two institutions. Such a study, as has been explained, can not be taken as representative of the work of a dean of women throughout the college year inasmuch as the functions performed vary greatly with the season. On the other hand, it can probably be considered somewhat representative of the functions performed by deans at the same time of year in institutions of similar organization.

On a blank chart the time for fourteen days, from eight in the morning until twelve at night, was divided into units of fifteen minutes. On one side of the chart was the code consisting of Parts I and II. The symbols of Part I stood for various problems engaging the attention of the dean of women, such as social functions, student government, or housing. The symbols of Part II stood for the activity through which she dealt with those problems, such as attendance, interview, or correspondence. For example, Q in Part I indicated "Social Functions"; X in Part II indicated "Attendance in Person"; Y indicated "Correspondence." If the recorder spent time on a social function, she put Q in the proper space on the chart. If she attended the function in person, she added X, making the entry Q X; but if she corresponded about the function, she wrote Q Y. Only time spent in specific duties for the college was recorded.

One chart was kept by Dean Anna Eloise Pierce of New York State College for Teachers, Albany, N. Y. The dean herself lives in the dormitory, which she is conducting as an experiment in college housing. She supervises the housekeeping and social life. For fourteen days, from May 30 till June 12, the dean's activities were recorded by her secretary who worked in her office and lived in the dormitory with her. The total number of hours accounted for was 146.25; the average number per day, 10.4.

The second chart was kept by Dean Lydia Jones of the State College for Teachers, Ypsilanti, Michigan. This institution has 2,200 women and 200 men. Since there are no dormitories, all students live in private homes, sorority houses, or boarding houses. The dean's staff consists of an assistant dean, a part-time social director, a part-time inspector of houses, a secretary, and paid chaperons for social functions.

It had been arranged that the dean's secretary should keep the chart for her, but this was found to be impractical as she was so busy she could not keep track of the activities of the dean of women; so the dean herself made the entries. Inasmuch as the dean was obliged to be absent from the college on personal business for a large part of two days, she kept the record, in order to give a better picture, for fifteen days instead of fourteen. The time was June 1 to 15, inclusive. Even so, the total amount of time accounted for was 129 hours, making an average for the fifteen days of 8.6 hours.

The keeping of the record by the dean herself may be criticized as follows:

1. Fifteen minutes is too large a unit of time, inasmuch as a dean may perform six different duties in fifteen minutes. She frequently has six two-minute interviews in that time. The recorder conceded, however, that larger spaces on the chart in which to make the record for each fifteen minutes would in a measure meet this objection.

2. Fifteen minutes at other times seemed too small a unit for purposes of accuracy. The recorder found it difficult to recall her activities so minutely after an interval of many hours.

3. The analysis of each act into "problem" and "activity" dealing with problem, the finding of the symbol for each, and the combination of the two (e.g., Q X for "Social Function, Attendance in Person") is too difficult for the short time the dean of women can spend in recording. In many cases, as the record shows, she put only one symbol in an entry. It was noticeable, however, that during the second week the recorder, having memorized the symbols, used both parts of the code in the entry.

4. The directions should state more explicitly just what is to be recorded. Actually, the dean of women gave more time to the college than she indicated, inasmuch as during the time for meals, which she always left vacant on the chart, she ate on several occasions with groups of students who wished to discuss college problems.

In general, these criticisms seem to point to two conclusions, the first of which is that it is impracticable for a dean to make a scientific, comprehensive time study of her own work unassisted. Another person should be in the office for that purpose alone, should observe the activities of the dean of women when she is present, check up with her several times during the day in regard to the duties unobserved, and do most of the classification of the duties and all of the recording.

In case a person can not be assigned to this work and the dean of women must herself do the recording, better results could be obtained, and the task made easier by recording fewer kinds of duties. One might study, for instance, only the number and type of persons with whom interviews are held without recording at the same time the matters dealt with. The latter could be made the subject of a separate study; they certainly should be if the person who interviews is obliged to make the record.

Granting the validity of these objections, the writer notes that these findings constitute the only actual quantitative record we have of the activities of a dean of women in a coeducational institution during any part of the college year. The study is to be continued later at other seasons.

FINDINGS

Both deans maintained that the period during which the record was kept was not typical. Case I made in the fourteen days two overnight trips to New York; Case II was moving from one house to another. Nevertheless the two records show surprising similarity. There is for each an entire absence of academic duties. Each has at times taught in her institution while acting as dean, but has been obliged through pressure of duties to cease. Each is a member of a faculty council dealing with academic matters but is personally concerned with few. Each dean has heavy social duties connected with commencement. A study made during

TABLE XXXIII

Time-Study of the Duties of Two Deans

Case I. New York State College for Teachers, Albany, New York
Time: May 30 to June 12, inclusive
Case II. State Normal College, Ypsilanti, Michigan
Time: June 1 to 15, inclusive

Activity	Hours			
	Case I		Case II	
	Number of Hours	Per Cent	Number of Hours	Per Cent
Chaperonage in Person	5.25	3.6	—	—
Church Work	1.5	1.0	—	—
Correspondence (Housing)	9.00	6.1	—	—
Correspondence (Outside Organization)	9.25	5.6	—	—
Correspondence (Unclassified)	—	—	6.00	4.7
Discipline (Research)	—	—	4.75	3.7
Dormitory (Housekeeping)	1.25	.9	—	—
Dormitory (Social Duties)	1.5	1.0	—	—
Dormitory (Plans)	8.5	5.8	—	—
Excuse-Granting	—	—	6.75	5.2
Handbook for Freshmen (Writing)	.75	.5	—	—
Housing (Off-Campus)	1.75	1.2	1.50	1.2
*Interviews (Not Excuses)	50.25	34.2	42.50	32.9
Outside Organization (Planning)	10.75	7.3	3.00	2.3
Outside Organization (Attendance)	14.75	10.1	—	—
Planning Alone (for Work of Staff Attendance)	—	—	19.75	15.3
Reading in Dean's Field	12.50	8.5	—	—
Sick Faculty (Visiting)	8.00	5.5	1.75	1.4
Social Functions (Attendance)	9.50	6.5	27.00	20.9
Social Functions (Plans)	.75	.5	.25	.2
Sororities (Plans)	.75	.5	2.75	2.1
Student Government (Meetings)	—	—	10.75	8.3
Unaccounted for	—	—	.75	.6
Visitors (Entertainment)	.75	.5	.75	.6
Vocational Guidance (Investigation)	1.00	.7	.75	.6
Y. W. C. A. (Attendance)	—	—	—	—
Total	146.75	100	129.00	100

* Note that interviews are analyzed separately in Table XXXIV.

TABLE XXXIV

ANALYSIS OF THE DEANS' INTERVIEWS

TYPES OF PERSONS INTERVIEWED	CASE I		CASE II	
	Number of Hours	Per Cent	Number of Hours	Per Cent
Faculty	4.00	16.3	12.00	26.2
Housekeeper—Dormitory	5.75	23.5	——	——
Landladies	.25	1.0	6.75	15.9
Parents	1.75	7.1	.75	1.8
Staff	2.00	8.2	10.50	24.7
Students	10.75	43.9	12.50	29.4
Total	24.50	100.0	42.5	100.0

*SUBJECTS OF THE INTERVIEWS	CASE I		CASE II	
	Number of Hours	Per Cent	Number of Hours	Per Cent
Academic Matters	.75	1.5	——	——
Discipline....................	.75	1.5	7.5	17.7
Dormitory—Housekeeping	5.75	11.4	——	——
Housing—Landladies	.50	1.0	10.0	23.5
Outside Organizations	14.50	28.8	.5	1.2
Residence Hall (Proposed)	5.00	10.0	.5	1.2
Social Affairs	6.50	12.9	.5	1.2
Sororities	4.50	9.0	5.0	11.7
Student Government	12.00	23.9	18.5	43.5
Total	50.25	100.0	42.5	100.0

*Note that these interviews are independent of the granting of excuses to which Case II gave 5.2 per cent of her time.

the weeks preceding examinations would very likely show fewer social duties. Each spends almost a third of her time in interviews, and the subjects of the interviews are strikingly similar. Each is concerned with off-campus housing, outside organizations, and sororities.

Explanation of differences to be noted is as follows:

1. Case II spends a great deal more time on discipline and student government. Hers is a larger institution situated in a small town, and the administration can be kept in close touch with the students. Case I can not supervise so closely, for students are scattered over a large city.

2. Case II spends a large amount of time personally granting excuses though she has several people on her staff. These excuses are for absence from class, and the permissions relate to absence for week-ends or being out at night later than the time prescribed by student government. As a matter of fact, the dean chooses to grant the excuses as a means of individual contact with the girls, and she considers this one of her most important duties inasmuch as the college has no dormitories to help in the regulation of social life and the landladies with whom the students live are unwilling and unable to place restrictions upon their boarders. Since the institution is near a university largely attended by men, the young women have a varied social life and the institution assumes a paternalistic attitude.

3. Case I spends twelve and one-half hours on reading in the dean's field while Case II spends none. The former reads during her train trips to New York.

4. Case II spent 17 per cent of the time working for outside organizations allied to the work of a dean of women.

The study thus far is of value, first, as a beginning toward a time-study of the work performed by a dean and, second, as corroborative of the findings in Chapter X in regard to the importance of the interview, work with student government, and social activities in the work of deans of women.

CHAPTER XII

VOCATIONAL GUIDANCE FOR PROSPECTIVE DEANS

For women who plan to fill positions as deans in colleges or universities there appear to be four essentials: certain personal qualifications, adequate education, a background of experience, and vocational opportunity. It is inadvisable for women to spend time, energy, and money preparing for this responsible vocation if they do not have suitable natural gifts, can not equip themselves properly, are handicapped by inexperience, or can not find vocational opportunity appropriate to their years and qualifications. It is, therefore, highly important that direct and frank vocational advice be given to prospective deans. To this end the data from vocational histories in Chapters V to IX and the analysis of duties in Chapter X will be of assistance.

PERSONAL QUALIFICATIONS

It is difficult to decide what are adequate personal qualifications for a dean. A great deal has been said on the subject. More especially is this true of the qualifications of the social dean or dean of women. Because of the variety of her duties and the publicity accorded her work as the result of professional courses for training this type of dean, her qualifications have furnished the theme for many bursts of eloquence. It is easier for a speaker when addressing deans of women to let his fancy play and to describe the ideal dean than it is for him to discuss the objectives and techniques of a dean's work. Usually such speakers describe a paragon in whom all the gifts and graces ever found in womankind are combined with the virtues commonly thought of as masculine. Sometimes the speaker has in mind some one of the three or four leading women educators in the country. The inference drawn is that only such women should be admitted to the professional courses for deans. By such descriptions very capable, modest women are sometimes kept from entering the vocation.

This powerful emphasis on a discouraging array of attributes essential to the ideal dean is, of course, the result of the realization of the importance of the dean's work. It is well to have that importance realized; it is well to hold up as an ideal to deans the finest type of woman educator; but, at the same time, it is necessary to keep in mind certain practical aspects concerning the qualifications of deans.

The first is that even if it were desirable to fill all deanships with the type of woman usually described, it would not be possible. Only two or three such women are born during a generation, whereas there are already 394 colleges and universities requiring deans. The work of deans must go on while standards in the vocation are being raised.

The second consideration is that a standardization of the personal qualities of deans would not be desirable even if it were possible. Deans are needed from coast to coast for the daughters of poor mountain whites and the daughters of our most distinguished citizens. It is seldom that the same woman would be acceptable to all communities.

The geographical location of an institution, its charter, its relation to state and church, its finances, traditions, and the social and academic background of its students are all factors which bear upon the type of dean which it seeks. The writer recently visited two successful deans in neighboring institutions, quite different in personality and native gifts. One, a glowing, exuberant type, owes a great part of her success in a university to skill in administration upon a large scale and the ability to move large groups of students through public addresses. The other, a shy little Quakeress, wins respect in a small college by her masterly grasp of detail and wins affection by untiring personnel work with students. Each dean remarked that she would not be successful in the other's position; each expressed her willingness to be used in this discussion as an example of *à chacun sa place*. In the work of deans in institutions of higher learning, there is undoubtedly evolving a certain degree of uniformity but such uniformity does not make inevitable or desirable a perfectly standardized type of dean.

Certain minimum essentials for the majority of deans there may be in appearance, manners, intelligence, and qualities of character. It has been proposed in the determination of such essentials that we might make a scale for rating deans; but until we have progressed much farther in the study of qualities of personality and character, we can hardly use such a scheme satisfactorily.

There remains, however, the immediate necessity of helping women to decide on their own qualifications for the work. To these we suggest that they note the duties outlined in Chapter X and examine in a sensible way their own qualifications with reference to the performance of such duties.[1]

From the time-studies in Chapter XI, aspirants to the deanship can get some idea of the day's work of the type of dean, and can decide whether in such work they would feel satisfied and successful. For example, from even so short a time-study as this, the young woman who enjoys books more than people will see that this is not the profession for her. A person with a one-track mind who can not turn her attention with ease from one task to another would hardly enjoy the work of a dean of women. Certain powers, of course, develop as one gets into the work and for such development some allowance should be made in the analysis of attributes.

A would-be dean will do well to seek advice concerning her own qualifications from teachers of professional courses for deans. From their acquaintance with many deans and with the needs of the field these teachers can often estimate the potentialities of those whom they advise.

The matter of age must receive consideration. As nearly as can be estimated from the data assembled, fifty per cent of the deanships investigated received their appointment as dean between the ages of twenty-eight and thirty-nine. Naturally the personal equation must always be considered. The women of twenty-five who in appearance and judgment seem to be thirty-five, the woman of fifty-five who appears to be forty, may each be called to a deanship. The woman of fifty-five, will, however, need to have some particularly strong asset, such as experience as a dean. In general, extreme youth and advanced years are disadvantageous to persons entering the vocation.

Religious affiliation is another factor which may have an important bearing on one's prospects in securing a position. We note from Table XXVII that, in general, deans are members of churches. It is likely that an avowed agnostic or atheist would find it

[1] For a suggestive list of qualifications see Merrill and Bragdon, *The Vocation of Dean.*

difficult to secure an appointment as dean in any type of college or university. We also note that, in general, an institution under church control tends to appoint a dean of its own sect. A prospective dean might find that her particular affiliation would limit the number of opportunities open to her.

EDUCATION

An examination of the principal duties of the dean (Chapter X) indicates that for any one of the three types of deanship a broad cultural background is necessary. A dean with a superficial education or a narrow specialized training can not properly as an administrative dean meet with trustees, approve appointments to the faculty, or guide educational policies. She can not as an academic dean interview girls on all sorts of academic problems unless her scholastic experience has been thorough and varied. As a social dean in a coeducational institution she can not, as a rule, provide a cultural background for young women unless she has had such a background.

The woman who has had a nondescript type of education, who has had to take courses not because they were valuable in content but because they were scheduled on Saturday or in the evening and gave credit toward a degree; the woman who has succeeded as a teacher though she has had no time in her life for music, art, or drama—that woman deserves admiration for her success but ought not, it would seem, to be a dean. The shrewd appraiser of qualifications looks to see not only whether a woman has the A.B. degree, held by 91 per cent of deans, but how, where, and under what circumstances it was earned. He realizes, too, that a woman with no degree may be more cultivated and more truly educated than another with three degrees.

As we have explained, varying types of personality are needed for deanships, particularly for those in coeducational institutions; but in regard to the culture and the thoroughness of the dean's education there appears to be a certain uniformity of demand. In spite of the current emphasis upon the extra-curricular aspects of education, colleges and universities are still considered the strongholds of culture; they are still supposed to exist chiefly for the sake of learning. Certainly the dean, who is one of the chief members of the faculty in such institutions, should have culture and learning worthy of respect.

Education beyond the Bachelor's degree will vary somewhat with the type of deanship toward which a person is looking. Among the academic deans in Group I, 70 per cent have the Doctor's degree; more than half were college teachers before they were deans; 70 per cent teach while acting as dean. Of the six administrative deans, three have the Doctor's degree; four were formerly college teachers; three still teach. A young woman who desires one of these two types of deanship had better take a Doctor's degree in a special field and begin to teach in college as soon as possible. The salaries paid to these deans are larger than those paid to deans in coeducational institutions; therefore the financial return will probably justify the expenditure in case one must think of financial return. If she does not become a dean, she will probably become a professor in her chosen field. In case a deanship is achieved, it will probably be the last step in an academic career begun with a genuine zest for the academic life.

As special preparation for the work of academic or administrative dean, a young woman would do well to add to her work in her special field a course in college administration. Such a course dealing with charters of institutions, finance, staff, curriculum, honors courses, personnel work, and the like, will give her information that otherwise could be obtained only through years of experience.

Therefore, to the college sophomore, who hopes some day to become an academic or administrative dean and is undecided whether to specialize at present in physics or history we give this advice: Specialize in the field in which you are most interested. It is true that it is more difficult for women to advance in physics than in history since men are often given the preference for positions in scientific fields. It is also true that if the deans of the future teach in addition to performing other duties, specialization in physics may prevent your becoming a dean, for the work of a dean is not compatible with long hours in a laboratory. On the other hand, you may marry and never teach, or you may wish to be a teacher and not a dean. In that case, it is far better to be thoroughly prepared in that field in which you are interested and gifted. Work for your Doctor's degree in that field. Obtain professorial rank in a college if possible. If a call to a deanship seems imminent, spend a sabbatical year or a summer session in a university school of education and take a professional course in college administration and other courses dealing with the problems of higher education.

For the woman who looks toward a deanship in a coeducational institution the problems of her advanced education are more complicated because the duties are more varied, the salaries appear to be smaller, and it is probable that conditions in the profession will in ten years be quite different from those of the present day. At present, of 84 deans of women in coeducational institutions in Group I, 79 per cent have been teachers; 40 per cent have taught in colleges; and 60 per cent still teach while they are deans. A certain number, percentage unknown, revert to teaching after being deans. Seventeen per cent of those in the group have the Doctor's degree. The higher the standing of the institution and the better the salary, the more likely is the dean of women to have that degree. In view of these facts, it appears wise for prospective deans of women who are genuinely interested in scholarship and can afford time and money to take the Doctor's degree in a special field and add to this the professional training for deans.

The Doctor's degree, it appears, had better be taken in a teaching subject for which there is likely to be a demand in almost any college or university, and which will not exact too much of the dean's time in the way of research. If the degree is taken in education with specialization in the work of a dean, the student must see to it that she is competent when her course is completed to teach some one phase of education. As a prospective dean she takes, let us say, a few courses in philosophy of education and educational psychology. As preparation for the work of dean those subjects are adequate; as preparation for teaching either subject, they are not. In the teaching field she must compete with persons who have concentrated all their graduate work on a particular phase of education. She would, however, especially after having had experience as dean of women in a college or university, be qualified to give a professional course for deans and workers in allied fields. For such courses there is a demand.

A Doctor's degree in any subject requires seven years of college and university work. This preparation is too expensive for a profession paying at present in coeducational institutions a median salary of $2,766. It is too long and laborious for the majority of deans of women. To them other advice must be given.

If, therefore, an undergraduate feels that she would like to work toward a deanship in a coeducational institution, we may advise her as follows: At present your most direct path to a position as dean of women is through college training. Get a sound liberal education. Be sure to take some work in psychology and sociology which will be related to your work as dean of women. Specialize in the academic subject that interests you most. Presumably, as a teacher in a college you must have a Master's degree, that is, at least one year more in your special subject than is required of the undergraduate whom you teach. Do as much advanced work in the subject as your means and ability permit. Become, if possible, a teacher in a college. Then, when the need arises, take professional training for the work of a dean of women.

If, during the next few years, there shall be a decided increase in the number of women who do not teach after they become deans, we shall give different advice to the next generation of undergraduates. We may instead advise them not to specialize in a teaching subject, but to concentrate all their graduate work upon professional training for a deanship.

EXPERIENCE

At present the most frequently travelled path to a deanship is teaching. Eighty per cent of all the deans in this investigation, be it remembered, were once pedagogues. According to precedent, a young woman could hardly be an academic or an administrative dean if she had not been a teacher. For social deans other types of experience are sometimes acceptable. It is well to have had experience in a field, such as social work or the Y.W.C.A., which has to do directly with the welfare of human beings.

There undoubtedly should be some sort of professional experience before coming to a deanship. Only one woman in Group I, we noted, had had no professional experience of any sort before she became a dean. In years of professional experience Q_1 for all institutions was 6.5; the median, 10,6; Q_3, 17.2. (See page 42.) The number of years of experience claimed by deans in women's colleges was greater than that of those in coeducational colleges.

In addition to professional experience, a dean should have enjoyed association with as many types of people as possible, and with young people in particular.

Vocational Opportunity

There are already, we have noted, 384 institutions requiring deans. Fifty per cent of the deans in this investigation have been in their positions less than three years, and over 20 per cent only one year. Seventy-eight per cent had no experience as college dean before taking their positions. From these facts the vocational opportunity would appear good. Several studies properly spaced as to time will actually have to be made before we can give a proper estimate of the annual turnover in this occupation.

We do know that at present the opportunities appear to cluster in certain parts of the country. Since the East has been settled longer and has more colleges, it has more deans. In the State of New York there are fourteen institutions approved by the Association of American Universities which have a dean; in Wyoming there is one; in California there are six.

Since the East is more conservative in educational policies, it has fewer institutions with deans who have had professional training. Of the 107 institutions in Group I, twenty-one have a dean of women who has taken or audited a professional course for deans, but only seven are in institutions east of Ohio. As we go West, we find more interest in professional training but fewer institutions. The geographical situation and the academic standing of institutions may have a distinct bearing upon a prospective dean's vocational opportunity unless she is willing and able to go to any part of the country or to any type of institution.

If a woman is willing to begin as assistant to a dean, the opportunities open to her are much more frequent. It is often wise for one without experience to begin as an assistant and she may, as an assistant dean in a university, have as interesting work as she would as dean in a small college.

For prospective deans of women there are also positions in allied fields, such as social service or Y.W.C.A. work, for which their training gives excellent preparation. At present the indications are that the woman of strong academic qualifications is more likely to find opportunity as an administrative, academic, or social dean in a college or university. The woman without them is likely to find her place in some other field which has elements in common with the work of a dean.

CHAPTER XIII

PROFESSIONAL TRAINING FOR DEANS OF WOMEN

It appears that the work of deans of women has taken its place among the professions, for it now has the three characteristics which differentiate a profession from a mere vocation. First, like the practice of law or medicine, it demands a sound liberal education as a basis for professional training. Ninety-one per cent of deans, we have seen, hold the Bachelor's degree. Second, it requires a special professional training for the duties to be performed. The number of courses offered and the large enrollment in these courses show how keenly the need for training is felt. Third, this vocation, the writer learned from interviews, is rapidly evolving an ethical code in accordance with which deans perform their duties. In regard to matters such as the conduct of the interview, the division of work among subordinates, and the coöperation to be effected between the dean and other officers of the institution, ethical principles are evolving, which, though not stated in print, are nevertheless being incorporated into the dean's practice.

PROFESSIONAL TRAINING FOR DEANS

Granting that the dean's work is a distinct profession we must next consider what sort of professional training will best prepare for it. From the analysis of the duties in Chapter X it appears that the training may well differ for different types of deans. For the administrative and academic deans we have advocated courses in college administration. Such a course, to the writer's knowledge, is offered in two institutions, in the summer session of the University of Chicago, and at Teachers College, Columbia University, during the summer and throughout the year. For deans of women, or social deans, a different type of training is necessary.

Courses for Deans of Women and Advisers of Girls. For this type of dean there are a larger number of professional courses offered. The most recent list is found in the *Yearbook of the National Association of Deans* for 1926. According to that report, twenty-four institutions offer courses for deans and advisers of women students. Of these courses one is in a technical and agricultural school, five are in colleges for teachers, two in colleges of liberal arts, and seventeen in universities. In eleven institutions the course is given only in the summer session. In eight instances the course is part of a planned series leading to a major. In nine institutions the course links with the social and extra-curricular activities for practice. In one university the Master's degree and the Doctor's degree may be taken in the field of advisers of women.

Objections Raised to Professional Training. Against these courses many objections have been raised by educators just as in years past opposition was brought against the idea of training in law, medicine, journalism, and other professions. Any new type of work which seeks recognition as a profession is at first grudgingly received by other professions. In some countries to-day lawyers have higher social standing than surgeons because lawyers were professional men when physicians were mere barbers employed to "let blood." Naturally persons who have known only a few deans of women and have observed them as doers of odd jobs about institutions can not conceive of the dean as a professional expert requiring a body of professional subject matter for the performance of her duties.

Advantages of Professional Training. As a matter of fact, we have not at present any statistics scientifically gathered which prove that a professionally trained dean of women, other qualifications being approximately equal, is more efficient than the one without such training. As time goes on, we shall look for proof from the testimony of administrators in regard to the relative merits of the professionally trained dean and the one who has never had training, and concerning the relative efficiency of a given dean before and after training. We shall look also to data presented by college surveys which include the department of the dean of women in their appraisal of the efficiency of a given institution.

At present it appears logical to conclude that professional training tends to diminish waste of time for the dean and to make her more efficient upon the commencement of her duties than she would otherwise be. Let us take, for example, the approval of plans and equipment of dormitories. If a dean is bright and energetic, it is argued, she can get for herself the information about dormitories; she does not need to take a course to acquire it.

It is true that there have been deans who, by dint of their own good sense and hard work have planned excellent residences for their institutions, though they have had no training for the task. They have been able to acquire the information necessary for the performance of their duties while they were serving as deans of women. Less and less frequently, however, can this be done. First, because this busy modern world is impatient, less disposed to wait for the person who must catch up with her job and, second, because the educational world is raising higher standards for the performance of tasks.

In the matter of college residences, institutions are raising standards. They will no longer tolerate a dormitory so built and equipped that the sound of ordinary conversation is nerve-wrecking, a dormitory with storage space so inadequate that students are obliged to keep their trunks in small study bedrooms, a dormitory in which the number of bathtubs is sadly disproportionate to the number of students, or one in which dining room and kitchen are so far separated that students rarely get a hot meal. After institutions have waited for years for much-needed residence halls, they are unwilling to make architectural mistakes which will handicap their students for generations. A dean of women is frequently asked immediately after appointment to give assistance to architects in planning buildings for women students. However brilliant and capable she may be, she is likely to give better assistance if she has studied housing under expert guidance. In regard to other duties, instances might be multiplied which would illustrate further the advantage of having acquired certain knowledge before accepting appointment as a dean.

In addition to saving time for its graduates and making them more efficient, the professional course improves standards for all deans of women. If each dean starts out alone, unprepared technically, she blunders along and years may pass before she can add much that is new to the common store of knowledge relative to the profession. If she comes from the professional course cognizant of the practices of the best deans of women in the country she can more quickly develop new techniques and add her experience for the benefit of others. The level of the entire profession is raised.

From professional training, too, there grows up an *esprit de corps,* a camaraderie, a professional spirit that helps both the individual and the workers as a whole. Often a woman who enters an important administrative position has a sense of isolation. She frequently finds that the president is the only person on the campus who understands the nature and importance of her duties, although, because of the nature of her duties, she must coöperate with most of the persons of influence in the institution. If a woman has taken a professional course for deans she feels less isolated. She continues to have contact with her former fellow-students who are now as deans meeting problems similar to her own. From these people she gets practical suggestions in regard to her work and a certain stimulus which is beneficial psychologically.

Another advantage of the professional course is the opportunity it offers to ambitious, scholarly young women to do research in a new field not already overworked. The argument that professional training for deans is not conducive to high scholarship among deans is unsound. The argument runs thus: Deans of women, it is asserted, as important officers in colleges and universities should be distinguished for intensive scholarship. Intensive scholarship comes from intensive study in one field. Deans, because of the variety of their duties, must take work in several fields. Therefore, the objectors conclude, deans of women can not be scholars unless they have previously done scholarly work in an academic teaching subject.

In answer to this argument we admit that deans must have a general knowledge of the subject matter in a number of fields. But, after acquiring this subject matter, they can choose one small aspect of the dean's work for scientific investigation in the same way that a scholar in Greek concentrates upon the use of the aorist. The work of deans is in itself a field for advanced study.

Limitations of Professional Training. There are, in spite of these advantages, certain limitations of the professional course which should be pointed out to the prospective dean of women. The course can not, as has been stated, prepare for every duty a dean may have to perform. It can only deal with those duties which take a large amount of the time of a large percentage of deans.

Again, no training can make up for the absence of native gifts, a liberal education, and experience.

In support of this statement those who do not advocate professional training frequently cite the social duties performed by the majority of deans. "Can a professional course," they ask, "give a woman the fine manners which come from an inbred consideration for other people? Can it develop in her the charm, poise, and *savoir faire* required of the official hostess in an institution? Can it create the judgment and tact required for the adequate supervision of the relations of adolescent boys and girls?" The answer is, of course, "no."

Professional training will give the student information concerning the social duties which will be hers; it can interpret for her social problems which in many institutions are at present very acute; it can give her the best solution for those problems evolved by successful deans. But superior intelligence and the more elusive elements of personality must be present as a basis.

The same argument holds with reference to a sound liberal education and experience. For these, as well as for native gifts, professional training is no substitute. It can in no sense be considered a short-cut to a deanship.

The Organization of the Professional Course. Ideally the professional course for deans of women will have three divisions: subject matter, practice, and research. By subject matter we mean the fundamental educational principles underlying the work of the dean of women and the body of information necessary for the performance of the most important duties. Practice implies an opportunity to perform some of the duties while in training. Research should bring the possession of techniques which can be applied in the solution of the dean's problems.

In order to build a curriculum for deans of women, one should first make an analysis of the duties and then proceed to see under what functions the duties may be classed. From the analysis in Chapter X, we find that the duties most commonly performed by deans in institutions of highest rating fall into the following groups:

1. Counsel on personal problems of students
2. Coöperation with student government
3. Organization and oversight of extra-curricular activities
4. Oversight of academic progress of students
5. Handling of cases of bad behavior
6. Organization of housing and responsibility for it
7. Coöperation with religious forces of the community

8. Organization and direction of part-time employment of students
9. Coördination of interests of women in relation to policies of the institution
10. Interpretation of college policies to the public

With these as a guide the maker of the curriculum must decide what subject matter should be prerequisite for the course and what subject matter and technique should actually be taught in it.

Prerequisites. First, among the subjects fundamental to the work of a dean as well as to any type of educational work, is philosophy of education. It would seem unwise for deans to assume their professional responsibilities without first having considered the issues involved. Techniques, as such, unrelated to a consistent theory of education, are of small value.

Psychology as a basic subject is also important. As a teacher of good habits, the dean must understand thoroughly the psychology of learning. As a personnel worker, she must know how to analyze the individual. It is true that her institution will probably provide for the testing of intelligence by one expert, and for the diagnosis of mental difficulties by another; but the dean must have sufficient knowledge of psychology to enable her to coöperate with these experts.

The study of sociology we would also recommend to the prospective dean. In addition to studying the woman student as an individual, the dean must study her in relation to other people. Furthermore, the dean must see the institution with all its members in relation to the community, the nation, and the world itself. To her will come problems relating to vocations, amusements, and marriage, for which she can find no adequate solution without a thoughtful consideration of the relations of human beings to each other and to their environment. For a proper perspective for these problems the dean must have as a guide a more intensive and extensive understanding of social relationships than may be presented by public opinion in the community in which she works. A broad course in sociology should help her to acquire such understanding.

Three subjects, then, are prerequisite for the actual professional training for deans of women: philosophy of education, psychology, and sociology. The professional course should provide specific instruction about the functions performed by the dean.

Concerning each of the functions listed, the builder of the professional course must ask these questions:

What are the actual tasks performed?

For their performance what information is necessary?

What portion of the information will the prospective deans have before they come into the course?

What portion can they easily acquire for themselves?

What information and techniques must become part of the professional training?

Accurate answers to the questions will come chiefly through research.

After the research has been completed and the answers found, the maker of the curriculum will proceed to organize the information and technique to be acquired. Let us illustrate with reference to vocational guidance. Sixty-four per cent of the deans in coeducational institutions, we have discovered, give vocational information. They would hardly have the necessary facts when they come into the professional course. In the course they should learn the types of information most needed and the sources of information. True, the students in the course for deans can not learn how to make a scientific analysis of the individual, but they can learn how to assemble the data collected by psychologist, physician, and other experts, and to give vocational advice upon it. Techniques involved would be the assembling of records, the case study, and the interview.

In a few years, it is likely, each first-rate institution will have its vocational adviser just as it has its college physician. Until that time the dean will have to do rudimentary advisement; and the more she can learn about it during her training, the better for the institution to which she goes.

From these illustrations the reader can see that the curriculum of the professional course is not static. There are bound to be many changes in the next five years as the work of the dean progresses and as we obtain information about her duties.

PRACTICE FOR PROSPECTIVE DEANS

Classroom work, however, is not the only form of instruction that should enter into a professional course for deans. There should also be opportunity for practice. Just as the professional training of physicians has its interneship, so the training of deans should provide suitable opportunity for them to make under supervision practical application of the information they have acquired. Agencies through which practice work might be provided for prospective deans are: the dean's office, dormitories, social settlements, high schools, girl scout and Y.W.C.A. organizations.

RESEARCH FOR PROSPECTIVE DEANS

Research constitutes the third phase of work in the ideal course for deans of women. For this research two tools may be cited: foreign language and statistical method.

Foreign languages are desirable for a study of the guidance of women in other countries. Deans, socalled, are known only in the United States and England, yet guidance is given college women in other countries and often by methods worthy of emulation in the United States. There is much abroad that we can observe with profit. It would be well for us to know by what methods self-supporting residential halls of one country preserve an atmosphere of elegance and serenity although students pay only a small amount for their living. It would be profitable to discover why the university students of another country can dispense entirely with chaperons at dances with no deleterious effect, and how, in another, educators are gradually overcoming in girls the inferiority complex characteristic of women in that land. The unsolved problems with reference to women students in America make it imperative that we gather all the information we can concerning proper guidance of the youth of other countries.

Research of this type admittedly can not be undertaken by all prospective deans. But for research involving statistical method, any prospective dean can acquire training, and any dean, unless she is in an institution of small size, will find skill in statistical research of distinct advantage.

DURATION OF THE PROFESSIONAL TRAINING

As to the length of time which training for deans should require, it is impossible to be dogmatic. Surely for the acquisition of information and techniques for research and the performance of some practice work, one year of graduate study beyond the liberal arts course is a minimum allotment of time. The history of other professional courses leads us to expect, that, although at present the necessary training may be compressed into a year, as time goes on and professional subject matter becomes available, the training period will have to be lengthened first to two and then to three years. Just as the older forms of educational service are requiring the Doctor's degree as evidence of advanced professional training for the specific tasks performed, so we may expect that eventually the position of dean of women will require that degree.

Professional training for deans of women, we conclude, presupposes certain temperamental characteristics, a sound liberal education, and as broad an experience as possible. The training itself should consist of subject matter, practice, and research related to the duties most commonly performed by deans. The nature of the subject matter, practice, and research can only be determined by an investigation of the work of deans as the profession develops. There are, according to this investigation, some ten functions so frequently performed that they might serve as a basis for a course of study.

CHAPTER XIV

SUMMARY

This investigation, conducted by means of the interview, the questionnaire, and the time-study, appears to furnish evidence of distinct trends in the profession of dean.

We have obtained data indicating a tendency for colleges attended by women to have a dean. Ninety-three per cent of the institutions investigated have a woman performing that function. Though there are great differences in the importance of her status and the nature of her duties in different types of institutions, the fact is that a woman is definitely appointed in these institutions to represent the interests of women students. The higher the academic rank of the institution, the more likely it is to have a woman dean.

Another tendency we noted is that women of good academic equipment are appointed to these positions. Not only have 91 per cent taken the Bachelor's degree, but a large group have done graduate work. Fifty-seven per cent have the Master's degree and fifteen per cent the Doctor's degree. The higher the academic rank of the college, the more likely is the dean to have advanced degrees. An intensive study of the institutions approved by the Association of American Universities shows that many deans in those institutions have taken academic honors and have had the advantages of foreign travel. In that group a greater percentage of deans in the colleges for women have taken the Doctor's degree than have deans in coeducational institutions.

There is in all the colleges investigated a tendency to give the dean rank on the faculty and higher rank than other members of the faculty with the same degrees would be likely to achieve. Forty per cent of the deans, including all types, have the rank of professor.

One explanation of their academic rank is found in the tendency to recruit deans from the teaching profession and to assign to them teaching duties in addition to their work as deans. Eight out of ten deans have been classroom teachers before appointment to deanships. The most direct approach to any type of deanship is through college teaching. Seventy per cent of deans teach after appointment. There are indications, however, that as the work of the profession develops, deans, particularly deans of women, will not teach but will concentrate upon the duties of their office. The number of hours per week now taught by deans ranges from one to thirty-two. The median for 187 deans during the first semester is over six hours per week. It appears that the better the academic standing of the college, the fewer hours per week the dean is likely to teach. Deans in colleges for women come to their deanships almost entirely from the teaching profession. Deans of women in coeducational institutions, though usually teachers, sometimes come with a background of other experience, especially if it is related to the interests of girls.

Persons almost never come to a deanship without some previous experience as wage-earners. The length of previous experience among deans serving in colleges for women appears to be somewhat greater than for deans in coeducational institutions. As nearly as can be judged from the data at hand, fifty per cent of all deans are appointed between the ages of twenty-eight and thirty-nine years.

In 107 institutions of highest rank we find most deans are unmarried. Most of them are without dependents.

The majority are church members.

There is a distinct tendency to give the dean smaller remuneration than her status in the institution and the importance of her duties seem to warrant. Fifty per cent of deans are receiving an annual salary between $2,096 and $3,531. Twenty-five per cent are paid less than $2,766; and twenty-five per cent more than $3,531. Only fifteen deans, including all types, are paid more than $5,000. In respect to salary, five trends are evident:

The higher the academic standing of an institution, the higher the salary of the dean.

The higher the academic training of the dean, the higher her salary.

The larger the total enrollment of students in an institution, the higher the salary of the dean.

The larger the total enrollment of women students in a coeducational institution, the higher the salary of the dean.

Salaries of deans in colleges for women tend to be larger than those for deans of women in coeducational institutions.

An analysis of the duties performed by the deans in the institutions of highest academic rank indicates that there are in this group three types of deans corresponding to the three general types of college organization found in the group. These types are: the college for women affiliated with a university, the independent college for women, and the coeducational institution. The difference in work performed often appears to be one of quantity rather than of kind. We find, for example, all types of deans greatly concerned with personnel work and student government; but to determine how much first-hand contact each type of dean has with these kinds of work, we must have more research.

Some outstanding differences, however, appear from the results of this investigation. The deans in affiliated colleges perform more administrative duties; the deans in the independent colleges for women, more responsible academic duties; and the deans in the coeducational institutions, more duties intimately related to the social life of the students.

The duties of the dean of women appear to be expanding in scope. These deans are becoming administrative officers with expert assistants; they are giving advice to students on academic matters and are being given a voice in academic councils of the faculty; they are asked to take an important part in the interpretation to the public of the policies of the institution. The increasing pressure of their duties is bound to result in the centralization of many college interests of women in the office of the dean of women, cared for by a staff of expert assistants, or it will result in a decentralization of functions, the duties hitherto performed by the dean of women being assigned to persons of highly specialized training, as personnel worker, vocational adviser, and head of residence, who will be responsible only to the president. Present indications point to a centralization of functions in the office of the dean of women.

With the facts assembled as a guide, we can give certain advice to prospective deans. We can warn them to be sure that they have the temperament and inclination for the work. Their personal attributes should be appraised by those who know deans and their duties; they can test their inclinations by voluntary work with young women. For any type of deanship they should have a sound liberal education, taking, if possible, such subjects as philosophy, psychology, and sociology which have a direct bearing on the guidance of young women. As conditions are at present in the profession, they should do graduate work in a teaching subject and, if possible, enter college teaching. Later this graduate work should be followed by professional training for a deanship. For the administrative and academic deanships in colleges for women, professional training will take the form of a study of expert college administration; for deanships in coeducational institutions, it should be a course expressly designed for deans of women.

The three divisions of such a professional course, which at the moment appear to be essential, are subject matter, practice, and research.

For the curriculum of the course, the present investigation shows ten of the main classes of function which should be studied. Much more research, however, is needed. Each one of the functional processes in the dean's work should be analyzed in greater detail and a decision made on the basis of the analysis as to the information and techniques that should become a part of the course.

It is to be hoped that the deans of women now in office can encourage research in this profession and give to the public an accurate notion of the rapid developments in it. It is they who have brought the work into a professional status; it is they who, with their experience, as the work develops, can best break it up into its component parts so that special techniques may be developed; it is they who know best the spiritual and aesthetic aspects of the work which an investigation like this can never bring out. The data here assembled constitute simply a point of departure for further research which will give a clearer understanding of the work of this important educational profession.

APPENDIX

A. BIBLIOGRAPHY

B. A DIRECTORY OF ACCREDITED COLLEGES AND UNIVERSITIES HAVING A WOMAN DEAN

C. QUESTIONNAIRES

    I. QUESTIONNAIRE SENT TO THE PRESIDENT

    II. QUESTIONNAIRE SENT TO THE REGISTRAR

    III. VOCATIONAL HISTORY QUESTIONNAIRE SENT TO WOMEN DEANS

    IV. QUESTIONNAIRE SENT TO WOMEN DEANS FOR AN ANALYSIS OF THEIR DUTIES

D. TIME CHART FOR DEAN OF WOMEN

A

BIBLIOGRAPHY

ADMISSION OF STUDENTS

HAWKES, HERBERT E. "Intelligence Tests as One Basis for Admission to College." *Thirteenth Yearbook, National Association of Deans of Women,* 1926.

"New Harvard Admission Plan." *School and Society,* 17:713, June 30, 1923.

PROBST, CARRIE MAE. "The Consideration Given to School Recommendations for Admission to Goucher College." *Thirteenth Yearbook, National Association of Deans of Women,* 1926.

SANDISON, HELEN. "What Should be Determining Factors in Requirements for Admission to College Examinations?" *Thirteenth Yearbook, National Association of Deans of Women,* 1926.

"Selective Admission to Colleges by University of Chicago." *School and Society,* 19:377-81, March, 1927.

WALTERS, RAYMOND. "The Personal Interview as One Basis for Admission to College." *Thirteenth Yearbook, National Association of Deans of Women,* 1926.

EDUCATION OF WOMEN AND COLLEGE ADMINISTRATION

"A Student Personnel Department of the La Salle-Peru Township High School and La Salle-Peru-Oglesby Junior College." Bureau of Educational Counsel, La Salle, Illinois.

CARNELL, LAURA H. "Should the University Curriculum be Adjusted for Women Students?" *Thirteenth Yearbook, National Association of Deans of Women,* 1926.

CARLTON, F. T. "Personnel Problems in Colleges." *Educational Review,* 65:173-75, March, 1923.

CHARTERS, WERRETT W. "Reorganization of Women's Education." *Educational Review,* 62: 224-31, October, 1921.

CLARK, THOMAS A. "Advisory Systems for Students." *School and Society,* 17:85-90, January 27, 1923.

COMSTOCK, ADA L. "New Devices and Desires in Colleges for Women." *Addresses and Proceedings of the Sixty-third Annual Meeting of the National Education Association,* pp. 426-34, 1925.

FINLEY, JOHN H. "The Ideal College." *Education,* 35: 320-328, January, 1915.

FRANK, GLENN. "Humanizing Education." *Century Magazine,* 98:651-66, September, 1919.

GOODSELL, WILLYSTINE. *The Education of Women.* Macmillan Co., New York, 1924.

HARKNESS, MARY L. "The Education of the Girl." *Atlantic Monthly,* pp. 324-30, March, 1914.

HARRIS, M. ANSTICE. "Questionnaire on the Function of the College." *School and Society,* 11 :530, May 1, 1920.

HOPKINS, L. B. "Personnel Procedure in Education." *The Educational Record Supplement,* No. 3, October, 1926. The American Council on Education, Washington, D. C.

HOPKINS, L. B. "Personnel at Northwestern." *Journal of Personnel Research,* 1 :27, October-November, 1922.

HURT, H. W. *The College Blue Book.* F. J. Riley, Chicago, 1923.

KELLY, FREDERICK J. *The American Arts College.* Macmillan Co., New York, 1925.

KING, HENRY C. "What the College Stands For." *Association of American Colleges Bulletin,* Vol. III, No. 1, February, 1917, Chicago.

KIRKPATRICK, JOHN E. *The American College and Its Rulers.* The New Republic Press, 1926.

LEWIS, ERVIN EUGENE. *Personnel Problems of the Teaching Staff.* Century Co., New York, 1925.

McCONN, MAX. "Quantity Production in Higher Education." *Survey,* 48 :659-62, September 1, 1922.

McLEOD, ANNIE. "Should the University Curriculum be Readjusted for Women Students?" *Thirteenth Yearbook, National Association of Deans of Women,* 1926.

MEIKLEJOHN, ALEXANDER. *Freedom and the College.* Century Co., New York, 1923.

MEIKLEJOHN, ALEXANDER. *The Liberal College.* Marshall Jones, Boston, 1920.

SLOSSON, EDWIN E. *Great American Universities.* Macmillan Co., New York, 1910.

SYKES, FREDERICK H. "The Social Basis of the New Education for Women." *Teachers College Record,* 18: 226-42, May, 1917.

TALBOT, MARION. *The Education of Women.* University of Chicago Press, Chicago, 1910.

THE AMERICAN COUNCIL ON EDUCATION. *The Educational Record,* Vol. 8, No. 2, April, 1927, Washington, D. C.

THWING, CHARLES F. *The American College.* Platt and Peck, New York, 1914.

YOAKUM, C. S. "Plan for a Personnel Bureau in Educational Institutions." *School and Society,* May 10, 1919.

ZOOK, GEORGE F. *Higher Education, 1920-22.* U. S. Bureau of Education Bulletin, 1923, No. 34, Washington, D. C.

EDUCATIONAL AND VOCATIONAL GUIDANCE

ADAMS, ELIZABETH K. *Women Professional Workers.* Macmillan Co., New York, 1921.

ALLEN, FREDERICK H. *A Guide to the Study of Occupations.* Harvard University Press, Cambridge, Mass., 1921.

BLAKE, MAYBELLE B. *Guidance for College Women.* Appleton, New York, 1926.

BREWER, JOHN M. *The Vocational Guidance Movement.* Macmillan Co., New York, 1919.

BUREAU OF VOCATIONAL INFORMATION. *Vocational Guidance in Colleges,* February 1, 1923.

Vocational Guidance and Junior Placement. Children's Bureau Publication No. 149, Employment Service Publication A., Washington, D. C.

ELIOT, CHARLES W. "Value During Education of the Life-Career Motive." *Proceedings of the National Educational Association,* pp. 134-41, 1910.

ENSIGN, M. R. "Vocational Guidance in Universities." *School and Society,* 17:699-702, July 23, 1923.

FEDERAL BOARD FOR VOCATIONAL EDUCATION. *Bibliography on Vocational Guidance,* Washington, D. C., 1925.

FRYER, DOUGLAS. "Intelligence and Interest in Vocational Adjustment." *Pedagogical Seminary,* 30:127-51, June, 1923.

HARAP, HENRY. "A Course in Academic Guidance for College Students." *School and Society,* 8: 145-48, August 3, 1918.

HATCHER, O. LATHAM. *Occupations for Women.* Southern Women's Educational Alliance, 401 Grace American Building, Richmond, Va.

HOLLINGWORTH, HARRY. *Vocational Psychology,* Chapter X. Appleton, New York, 1916.

HUSBAND, RICHARD W. *Vocational Guidance and the College of Liberal Arts.* National Committee of Bureau of Occupations, New York, 1922.

HUSBAND, RICHARD W. "Vocational Guidance at Dartmouth." *School and Society,* 11:407-408, April 3, 1920.

KELLEY, TRUMAN L. *Educational Guidance.* Contributions to Education, No. 71. Teachers College, Columbia University, 1914.

KELLY, ROBERT L. "Vocational Distributions of College Graduates." *Association of American Colleges Bulletin,* Vol. VI, No. 2, pp. 12-33, October, 1920. 45 West 18th Street, New York.

KITSON, HARRY D. "A Preliminary Personnel Study of Psychologists." *Psychological Review,* 33:315 ff., July, 1926.

KITSON, HARRY D. *The Psychology of Vocational Adjustment.* J. B. Lippincott, Philadelphia, 1925.

KITSON, HARRY D. "The Scientific Compilation of Vocational Histories as a Method to be Used in Vocational Guidance." *Teachers College Record,* 28:50-57, September, 1926.

LAIRD, DONALD A. "The Careers of the College Student." *Pedagogical Seminary,* 30:347-57, December, 1923.

LEIGH, MILDRED B. "Vocational Guidance for College Women." *Educational Review,* 62:34-45, June, 1921.

MAVERICK, LEWIS A. *The Vocational Guidance of College Students.* Harvard University Press, Cambridge, Mass., 1926.

MICHELL, ELENE. "The Life-Career Motive and the Dean of Girls." *School and Society,* 20: 70-74, July 19, 1924.

NATIONAL VOCATIONAL GUIDANCE ASSOCIATION. *The Principles of Vocational Guidance.* Graduate School of Education, Harvard University, Cambridge, Mass.

PETERS, IVA L. "A Two-Year Experiment with Vocational Guidance in a Woman's College." *Pedagogical Seminary,* 30:225-40, September, 1923.

PIERCE, ANNA ELOISE. *Catalogue of Literature for Advisers of Young Women and Girls.* The H. W. Wilson Co., New York, 1921.

PROCTOR, WILLIAM M., *Educational and Vocational Guidance.* Houghton Mifflin and Co., Boston, 1925.

PRUETTE, LORINE. "Vocational Orientation for the College Student." *Educational Review,* 69:83-85, February, 1925.

ROGERS, AGNES L. "The Use of Psychological Tests in the Administration of Colleges of Liberal Arts for Women." *Journal of the American Association of University Women,* Vol. XV, No. 5, pp. 141-45, October, 1922.

SMITH, HELEN H. "College Life and Its Training for Functioning after Graduation." *Eleventh Yearbook, National Association of Deans of Women,* 1924.

STONE, H. E. "Guidance Activities of American Colleges and Universities." *Industrial Arts Magazine,* 12:283, July, 1923.

STONE, WILLIAM H. "Vocational Guidance in Colleges and Universities." *Twenty-third Yearbook, National Society for the Study of Education,* Part II, pp. 139-45. Public School Publishing Co., Bloomington, Ill., 1924.

WILEY, EDGAR J. "Organizing the Liberal Arts College for Vocational Guidance." *National Vocational Guidance Association Bulletin,* Vol. I, No. 9, pp. 143-46, April, 1923.

WOOD, BEN D. "College Curricula and Vocational Guidance." *School and Society,* 21:508-12, April 25, 1925.

WOOLLEY, HELEN T., "New Opportunities for College Women." *Association of American Colleges Bulletin,* Vol. 3, No. 3, pp. 117-31, April 1917.

HEALTH

COMSTOCK, ADA L. "Health and College Routine." *School and Society,* October 11, 1924.

WOMEN'S FOUNDATION FOR HEALTH. *Survey of Student Health Service in the United States.* New York.

HOUSING

KUNKEL, FLORENCE. "To What Extent Should the Dean of Women Function in Dormitory Management?" *Thirteenth Yearbook, National Association of Deans of Women,* 1926.

MINROW, MAUDE E. "How Housemothers May Aid in the Betterment of the Living Conditions of Students and Their Effect upon Character and Morals." *Thirteenth Yearbook, National Association of Deans of Women,* 1926.

NEWMANN, A. EVELYN. "Student Living Conditions and Their Effects on Character and Morals." *Thirteenth Yearbook, National Association of Deans of Women,* 1926.

Scales, Laura B. "The New College Houses." *Smith College Quarterly,* November, 1922.

Talbot, Marion. "Dormitory Life for College Women." *Journal of Home Economics,* 2:490-95, November, 1910.

Tufts, Edith G. "Organization of the Work of the Head of Halls." *Proceedings of the National Association of Deans of Women,* Vol. 60, 1922.

ORIENTATION OF COLLEGE FRESHMEN

Boraas, Julius. "Troubles of College Freshmen." *School and Society,* 6:491-94, October 27, 1917.

Brown, Mary L. "Talks to Freshmen—Their Content and Value." *Tenth Yearbook, National Association of Deans of Women,* 1923.

Doermann, Henry J. *The Orientation of College Freshmen.* Williams and Wilkins, Baltimore, 1926.

English, A. C. "How Shall We Instruct the College Freshmen in the Use of the Library?" *School and Society,* 24:110-11, July 24, 1926.

"Freshman Week at University of Maine." *School and Society,* 21:23-24, January 3, 1925.

Good, C. V. "Freshman Week at Miami University." *School and Society,* 24:614, November 13, 1926.

Hansen, Albert A., "The Freshman Adviser." *School and Society,* 5:200, February 17, 1917.

Ho, C. J. "How Freshmen Find Themselves (or Don't)." *Educational Review,* 71:29-36, January, 1926.

Jameson, Kate and Lockwood, Frank C. *The Freshman Girl.* D. C. Heath, New York, 1925.

Jones, A. L. "Freshmen, Examination, and Placement." *School and Society,* 1:444-49, April 11, 1925.

Kingsley, Julius S. and Williams, Gardner. "An Outline for an Orientation Course for Freshmen." *Middlebury College Bulletin,* Vol. 20, No. 1, July, 1925.

Little, C. C. "Freshman Week." *School and Society,* 24:765, December 18, 1926.

Pierce, Anna E. "Helping the Freshman Women to Make an Early and Successful Adjustment to Their New Environment." *Tenth Yearbook, National Association of Deans of Women,* 1923.

Stimson, Dorothy. "The Best Method of Adjusting the Freshman to College." *Tenth Yearbook, National Association of Deans of Women,* 1923.

Stoddard, G. D. "Orientation Programs for College Freshmen." *School and Society,* 20:370, September 30, 1924.

Stoddard, G. D. "Status of Freshmen in Large Universities." *School and Society,* 24:586-89, November 6, 1926.

Wilkins, Ernest H. "Freshman Week at the University of Chicago." *School Review,* 32:746-51, December, 1924.

PERSONAL PROBLEMS OF STUDENTS

Allport and Allport. "Personality Traits, Their Classification and Measurement." *Journal of Abnormal Psychology,* Vol. 16, 1921.

BUELL, BRADLEY. "Interviews, Interviewers, and Interviewing." *The Family,* 6:86-90, July, 1925.

BURNHAM, WILLIAM H. *The Normal Mind.* Appleton, New York, 1925.

BURNHAM, WILLIAM H. *Great Teachers and Mental Health.* Appleton, New York, 1926.

CABELL, ELVIRA D. "The Dean's Social Conferences with Students: What They Should Include and Accomplish." *Tenth Yearbook, National Association of Deans of Women,* 1923.

CLARK, THOMAS A. *Discipline and the Derelict.* Macmillan Co., New York, 1922.

CLOW, LUCIA B. "The Art of Helping Through the Interview." *The Family,* 6:129-32, May, 1925.

CONRAD, ELIZABETH. "The Maladjusted Girl." *Thirteenth Yearbook, National Association of Deans of Women,* 1926.

FITCH, FLORENCE M., "Principles of Social Conduct." Pamphlet prepared by a committee of deans of women. Oberlin, Ohio.

GROVES, ERNEST R. *Personality and Social Adjustment.* Longmans, Green, and Co., New York, 1925.

HEALY, WILLIAM,*Mental Conflicts and Misconduct.* Little, Brown and Co., Boston, 1917.

KITSON, HARRY D. *The Scientific Study of the College Student.* Princeton University Press, 1917.

KITSON, HARRY D. "A Shift of Emphasis Needed in Personnel Research." *Journal of Applied Psychology,* 6:141-148, June, 1922.

KNIGHT, F. B. "The Effect of Acquaintance Factor Upon Personal Judgments." *Journal of Educational Psychology,* 14:129ff., March, 1923.

LEATHERMAN, ZOE E. and DOLL, EDGAR A. *A Study of the Maladjusted College Student,* Ohio State University Press, Columbus, Ohio, 1925.

PRATT, G. L. "Personality and Social Adjustments of College Students." *Speech Education,* 10:364-6, 8, November, 1924.

RANDALL, OTIS E. "Character Building in College." *Education,* 35: 620-27; June, 1915.

RONAN, BERTHA. "Social Conferences with Students: What They Should Include and Accomplish." *Tenth Yearbook, National Association of Deans of Women,* 1923.

SMITH, C. A. "Why Students Leave College." *Educational Administration and Supervision,* 9:339-44, September, 1923.

STURTEVANT, SARAH M. and HAYES, HARRIET. "The Use of the Interview in Advisory Work." *Teachers College Record,* 28:551-61, February, 1927.

TOOPS, HERBERT A. "Individual Guidance Card for Students." *School and Society,* 20:125-28, July 26, 1924.

WAITE, ALICE W. "The Difficulties of the Sophomore Year." *Tenth Yearbook, National Association of Deans of Women,* 1923.

RELIGION

ALVORD, KATHERINE S. "Religious Life in College and Its Training for Functioning after Graduation." *Eleventh Yearbook, National Association of Deans of Women,* 1924.

COE, GEORGE A. *"What Ails Our Youth?* Chas. Scribner and Sons, New York, 1924.

FITCH, ALBERT P. "Student Attitude To-day Toward Organized Morals and Religion." *Eleventh Yearbook, National Association of Deans of Women,* 1924.

WRIGHT, WILLIAM K. *The Student's Philosophy of Religion.* Macmillan Co., 1922.

PROBLEMS OF SCHOLARSHIP

COMSTOCK, ADA. "Time and the College Girl." *School and Society,* 21: 326-27, March 14, 1925.

"Honors Courses at Swarthmore." *Association of American Colleges Bulletin,* May, 1926.

JOHNSON, JOHN B. "New Demands for Differential Treatment of Students in the College of Liberal Arts." *The Association of American Universities, Journal of Proceedings and Addresses of the Twenty-sixth Annual Conference,* pp. 76-77. University of Chicago Press, Chicago, 1924.

LYMANN, R. L. "The Problem of Student Honor in Colleges and Universities." *School Review,* 35: 253-71, April, 1927.

MILLER, H. W. "Segregation on the Basis of Ability." *School and Society,* 26:84-88, July, 1927.

MILLER, H. W. "Segregation on the Basis of Ability, II." *School and Society,* 26: 114-20, July 23, 1927.

NARDIN, F. LOUISE. "Successful Means of Supervising the Scholarship of Freshman Women." *Tenth Yearbook, National Association of Deans of Women,* 1923.

SEASHORE, CARL E. "The Placement Examination as a Means for the Early Discovery and Motivation of the Future Scholar." *The Association of American Universities, Journal of Proceedings and Addresses of Twenty-seventh Annual Conference,* pp. 50-56. University of Chicago Press, Chicago, 1925.

SIMRALL, JOSEPHINE. "Ways of Promoting Scholarship." *Tenth Yearbook, National Association of Deans of Women,* 1923.

WOOD, BEN D. "The Sifting Out of the Exceptional Student and His Relationship to the University Curriculum." *The Association of American Universities, Journal of Proceedings and Addresses of the Twenty-fourth Annual Conferences,* pp. 32-39, 1922.

STANDARDIZATION OF HIGHER INSTITUTIONS

"Accredited Higher Institutions." *Educational Record,* April, 1925.

Association of American Universities, Journal of the Proceedings and Addresses of the Twenty-sixth Annual Conference, 1924. Accepted list of Colleges and Universities. Approved by the Association of American Universities.

JOHN, ELLA. "Academic Status of Women on University Faculties." *Journal of American Association of University Women,* 1924.

KOOS, LEONARD V. U. S. Bureau of Education, Bulletin, 1919, No. 15, p. 23. *Study of Standardizing Agencies.* U. S. Bureau of Education, Bulletin, 1926, No. 10.

ZOOK, GEORGE F. "The Movement Toward the Standardization of Colleges and Universities." *School and Society*, 16: 706-12, December 23, 1922.

STATUS AND DUTIES OF DEANS

"Academic Status of Women on University Faculties." *Journal of American Association of University Women*, 1924.

BARNARD, EDITH A. "Educational and Other Qualifications for Deans of Women." *Eleventh Yearbook, National Association of Deans of Women*, 1924.

CARPENTER, MIRIAM F. "Educational and Other Qualifications for Deans of Women." *Eleventh Yearbook, National Association of Deans of Women*, 1924.

DICK, G. S. "What a President May Rightly Expect from a Dean of Women." *Proceedings of the National Education Association*, 59: 395-97, 1918.

GLASS, META. "Address." *Thirteenth Yearbook, National Association of Deans of Women*, 1926.

HAWKES, HERBERT E. "Dean to Dean." *Thirteenth Yearbook, National Association of Deans of Women*, 1926.

JEWELL, MARY F. "Intra-Mural Activities; Constructive Relationships." *Tenth Yearbook, National Association of Deans of Women*, 1923.

MATTHEWS, LOIS K. *The Dean of Women*. Riverside Press, New York, 1915.

MERRILL, RUTH A. and BRAGDON, HELEN D. "The Vocation of Dean." Press and Publicity Committee of the National Association of Deans of Women.

PARK, MARION. "Address." *Thirteenth Yearbook, National Association of Deans of Women*, 1926.

RICHARDS, FLORENCE L. "The Teaching Load of a Dean of Women in a State Teachers College. What Shall It Be?" *Tenth Yearbook, National Association of Deans of Women*, 1923.

RICHARDS, FLORENCE L. "The Dean of Women." *American School Master*, 9:241.

STURTEVANT, SARAH M. "The Qualifications and Preparation of Deans of Women." *Eleventh Yearbook, National Association of Deans of Women*, 1924.

WHITE, GEORGIA L. "The Tests of Success in Our Work as Deans of Women." *Thirteenth Yearbook, National Association of Deans of Women*, 1926.

YOST, MARY. "The Extra-Mural Activities of a Dean of Women. What Shall They Be?" *Tenth Yearbook, National Association of Deans of Women*, 1923.

SOCIAL PROGRESS OF THE DEAN

ALGER, GEORGE W. "Leisure—For What?" *Atlantic Monthly*, 135: 483-92, April, 1925.

AMOS, THYRSA W. "Student Government." *Addresses and Proceedings of the Sixty-third Annual Conference of the National Education Association*, pp. 440-49, 1925.

BEAUMONT, AMANDA LEE. "Are Fraternities a Help or a Hindrance in a Teachers College?" *Thirteenth Yearbook, National Association of Deans of Women,* 1926.

BENJAMIN, C. H. "Student Activities." *School and Society,* 23: 231-34, February 12, 1926.

BREWSTER, ETHEL H. "Social Life as an Academic Problem." *Eleventh Yearbook, National Association of Deans of Women,* 1924.

BROOKS, WENDELL S. "Study of a Simple Typical Extra-Curricular Activity." *Educational Administration and Supervision,* Vol. 10, No. 3, November, 1924.

CHOPIN, F. STUART. "Extra-Curricular Activities of College Students." *School and Society,* 23:212-16, February 13, 1926.

DEALEY, HERMOINE L. "Problems of the College Sorority." *School and Society,* 4: 735-40; November, 1926.

GERLACH, MIRIAM. "How to Organize Student Government." *Thirteenth Yearbook, National Association of Deans of Women,* 1926.

HILLBOE, GERTRUDE. "Value of Student Organizations in Training for Citizenship." *Eleventh Yearbook, National Association of Deans of Women,* 1924.

JONES, GERTRUDE. "Three Principles Underlying the Administration of Extra-Curricular Activities." *The School Review,* 33: 510-22, September, 1925.

MEIKLEJOHN, ALEXANDER. "The Place of Student Activities." *Education.* 35: 312-19, January, 1915.

NEWTON, LUCY. "College Politics and Its Relations to Citizenship." *Eleventh Yearbook, National Association of Deans of Women,* 1924.

POMEROY, SARAH J. "The Service of the Women's Fraternities." *Independent,* 79:413-14, September 21, 1914.

PRUETTE, LORINE. *Women and Leisure.* Dutton, New York, 1925.

RICKERT, EDITH. "The Fraternity Idea Among College Women." *Century,* 63: 97-106, November, 1912.

ROSS, W. D. "Leisure as an Objective of Education." *Educational Review,* 66: 71-74, September, 1923.

SMITH, HELEN. "The Use of Penalties in Student Government." *Tenth Yearbook, National Association of Deans of Women,* 1923.

U. S. BUREAU OF EDUCATION. "List of References on Student Self-Government." United States Department of the Interior, Washington, D. C.

B

A DIRECTORY OF ACCREDITED COLLEGES AND UNIVERSITIES HAVING A WOMAN DEAN *

Institution	Location	Title
1. Adelphi College	Brooklyn, N. Y.	Dean of Women
2. Agnes Scott College	Decatur, Ga.	Dean
3. Agricultural College of Utah	Logan, Utah	Dean of Women
4. Alabama Polytechnic Institute	Auburn, Ala.	Dean of Women
5. Albion College	Albion, Mich.	Dean of Women
6. Alfred University	Alfred, N. Y.	Dean of Women
7. Allegheny College	Meadville, Pa.	Dean of Women
8. Alma College	Alma, Mich.	Dean of Women
9. Augustana College	Rock Island, Ill.	Dean of Women
10. Baker University	Baldwin, Kan.	Dean of Women
11. Baldwin-Wallace College	Berea, Ohio	Dean of Women
12. Barnard College	New York City	Dean
13. Bates College	Lewiston, Me.	Dean of Women
14. Baylor University	Waco, Texas	Dean of Women
15. Beloit College	Beloit, Wis.	Dean of Women
16. Bethany College	Bethany, W. Va.	Dean of Women
17. Birmingham Southern College	Birmingham, Ala.	Dean of Women
18. Boston University	Boston, Mass.	Dean of Women
19. Bradley Polytechnic Institute	Peoria, Ill.	Dean of Women
20. Brigham Young University	Provo, Utah	Dean of Women
21. Brown University	Providence, R. I.	Dean
22. Bryn Mawr College	Bryn Mawr, Pa.	Dean
23. Bucknell University	Lewiston, Pa.	Dean of Women
24. Butler College	Indianapolis, Ind.	Dean of Women
25. Capital University	Columbus, Ohio	Dean of Women
26. Carleton College	Northfield, Minn.	Dean of Women
27. Carnegie Institute of Technology	Pittsburgh, Pa.	Dean of Women
28. Carroll College	Waukesha, Wis.	Dean of Women
29. Carthage College	Carthage, Ill.	Dean of Women

* The author will be grateful for any correction to this list.

INSTITUTION	LOCATION	TITLE
30. Central College	Fayette, Mo.	Dean of Women
31. Coe College	Cedar Rapids, Ia.	Dean of Women
32. Coker College	Hartsville, S. C.	Hostess
33. Colby College	Waterville, Me.	Dean of Women
34. College of Emporia	Emporia, Kan.	Dean of Women
35. College of Idaho	Caldwell, Idaho	Dean of Women
36. College of Industrial Arts	Denton, Texas	Dean of Women
37. College of Mt. St. Vincent-on-the-Hudson	Mt. Vincent, N. Y.	Dean of Women
38. College of New Rochelle	New Rochelle, N. Y.	Dean
39. College of Puget Sound	Tacoma, Wash.	Dean of Women
40. College of St. Catherine	St. Paul, Minn.	Dean of Women
41. College of the City of Detroit	Detroit, Mich.	Advisers
42. College of St. Teresa	Winona, Minn.	Title Unknown
43. College of William and Mary	Williamsburg, Va.	Dean of Women
44. College of Wooster	Wooster, Ohio	Dean of Women
45. Colorado Agricultural College	Fort Collins, Colo.	Dean of Women
46. Colorado College	Colorado Springs, Colo.	Dean of Women
47. Columbia University	New York City	Adviser
48. Connecticut College for Women	New London, Conn.	Dean of Students
49. Converse College	Spartanburg, S. C.	Dean of Women
50. Cornell College	Mount Vernon, Iowa	Dean of Women
51. Cornell University	Ithaca, N. Y.	Dean of Women
52. Culver-Stockton College	Canton, Mo.	Dean of Women
53. Dakota Wesleyan University	Mitchell, S. C.	Dean of Women
54. Defiance College	Defiance, Ohio	Dean of Women
55. Denison University	Granville, Ohio	Dean of Women
56. De Pauw University	Greencastle, Ind.	Dean of Women
57. Dickinson College	Carlisle, Pa.	Dean of Women
58. Doane College	Crete, Neb.	Dean of Women
59. Drake University	Des Moines, Iowa	Dean of Women
60. Drury College	Springfield, Mo.	Dean of Women
61. Duke University	Durham, N. C.	Dean of Women
62. Earlham College	Richmond, Ind.	Dean of Women
63. Elmira College	Elmira, N. Y.	Dean of Women
64. Eureka College	Eureka, Ill.	Dean of Women
65. Florida State College for Women	Tallahassee, Fla.	Dean of Students
66. Franklin College	Franklin, Ind.	Dean of Women
67. Friends University	Wichita, Kan.	Dean of Women
68. Geneva College	Beaver Falls, Pa.	Dean of Women
69. George Washington University	Washington, D. C.	Dean of Women

INSTITUTION	LOCATION	TITLE
70. Georgetown College	Georgetown, Ky.	Dean of Women
71. Goucher College	Baltimore, Md.	Dean
72. Grinnell College	Grinnell, Iowa	Dean of Women
73. Grove City College	Grove City, Pa.	Dean of Women
74. Gustavus Adolphus College	St. Peters, Minn.	Dean of Women
75. Hamline University	St. Paul, Minn.	Dean of Women
76. Hanover College	Hanover, Ind.	Dean of Women
77. Harvard University	Cambridge, Mass.	Dean of Women
78. Hastings College	Hastings, Neb.	Dean of Women
79. Heidelberg University	Tiffin, Ohio	Dean of Women
80. Hillsdale College	Hillsdale, Mich.	Dean of Women
81. Hiram College	Hiram, Ohio	Dean of Women
82. Hood College	Frederick, Md.	Dean
83. Hope College	Holland, Mich.	Dean of Women
84. Howard College	Birmingham, Ala.	Social Directors
85. Howard University	Washington, D. C.	Dean of Women
86. Hunter College	New York City	Dean
87. Huron College	Huron, S. D.	Dean of Women
88. Illinois College	Jacksonville, Ill.	Dean of Women
89. Illinois Wesleyan University	Bloomington, Ill.	Dean of Women
90. Illinois Women's College	Jacksonville, Ill.	Dean of Women
91. Indiana University	Bloomington, Ind.	Dean of Women
92. Iowa State College of Agriculture and Mechanical Arts	Ames, Iowa	Dean of Women
93. Iowa Wesleyan University	Mt. Pleasant, Iowa	Dean of Women
94. James Millikan University	Decatur, Ill.	Dean of Women
95. Juniata College	Huntingdon, Pa.	Dean of Women
96. Kalamazoo College	Kalamazoo, Mich.	Dean of Women
97. Kansas State Agricultural College	Manhattan, Kan.	Dean of Women
98. Knox College	Galesburg, Ill.	Dean of Women
99. Lake Erie College	Painesville, Ohio	Dean of Women
100. Lake Forest College	Lake Forest, Ill.	Dean of Women
101. Laurence College	Appleton, Wis.	Dean of Women
102. Lebanon Valley College	Annville, Pa.	Dean of Women
103. Leland Stanford Junior University	Stanford University, California	Dean of Women
104. Lewis Institute	Chicago, Ill.	Dean of Women
105. Lindenwood College	St. Charles, Mo.	Dean of Women
106. Lombard College	Galesburg, Ill.	Dean of Women
107. Louisiana College	Pineville, La.	Dean of Women
108. Louisiana State University	Baton Rouge, La.	Dean of Women
109. Macalester College	St. Paul, Minn.	Dean of Women
110. Marietta College	Marietta, Ohio	Dean of Women
111. Marquette University	Milwaukee, Wis.	Advisers

INSTITUTION	LOCATION	TITLE
112. Massachusetts Agricultural College	Amherst, Mass.	Advisers
113. Maryville College	Maryville, Tenn.	Dean of Women
114. Marywood College	Scranton, Pa.	Dean of Women
115. McPherson College	McPherson, Kan.	Dean of Women
116. Miami University	Oxford, Ohio	Dean of Women
117. Michigan State College	East Lansing, Mich.	Dean of Women
118. Middlebury College	Middlebury, Vt.	Dean of Women
119. Mills College	Oakland, Calif.	Dean
120. Millsaps College	Jackson, Miss.	Dean of Women
121. Milwaukee-Downer College	Milwaukee, Wis.	Dean
122. Mississippi State College for Women	Columbus, Miss.	Dean of Women
123. Missouri Valley College	Marshall, Mo.	Dean of Women
124. Missouri Wesleyan College	Cameron, Mo.	Dean of Women
125. Monmouth College	Galesburg, Ill.	Dean of Women
126. Montana State College of Agricultural and Mechanical Arts	Bozeman, Mont.	Dean of Women
127. Moravian College for Women	Bethlehem, Pa.	Dean of Women
128. Morningside College	Sioux City, Iowa	Dean of Women
129. Mt. Holyoke College	South Hadley, Mass.	Dean
130. Mt. St. Joseph College	Dubuque, Iowa	Dean of Women
131. Mount Union College	Alliance, Ohio	Dean of Women
132. Municipal University of Akron	Akron, Ohio	Dean of Women
133. Muskingum College	New Concord, Ohio	Dean of Women
134. Nebraska Wesleyan University	University Place, Neb.	Dean of Women
135. New York State Teachers College	Albany, N. Y.	Dean of Women
136. New York University	New York City	Adviser
137. North Carolina College for Women	Greensboro, N. C.	Dean of Women
138. North Dakota Agricultural College	Fargo, N. D.	Dean of Women
139. Northwestern College	Naperville, Ill.	Dean of Women
140. Northwestern University	Evanston, Ill.	Dean of Women
141. Oberlin College	Oberlin, Ohio	Dean of Women
142. Occidental College	Los Angeles, Calif.	Dean of Women
143. Ohio State University	Columbus, Ohio	Dean of Women
144. Ohio University	Athens, Ohio	Dean of Women
145. Ohio Wesleyan University	Delaware, Ohio	Dean of Women

Institution	Location	Title
146. Oklahoma Agricultural and Mechanical College	Stillwater, Ohio	Dean of Women
147. Oklahoma College for Women	Chickasha, Okla.	Dean of Women
148. Oregon Agricultural College	Corvallis, Ore.	Dean of Women
149. Ottawa University	Ottawa, Kan.	Dean of Women
150. Our Lady of the Lake	San Antonio, Tex.	Dean of Students
151. Otterbein University	Waterville, Ohio	Dean of Women
152. Pacific University	Forest Grove, Ore.	Dean of Women
153. Park College	Parkville, Mo.	Dean of Women
154. Parsons College	Fairville, Iowa	Dean of Women
155. Penn College	Oskaloosa, Iowa	Dean of Women
156. Pennsylvania College for Women	Pittsburgh, Pa.	Dean of Women
157. Pennsylvania State College	State College, Pa.	Dean of College
158. Phillips University	East Enid, Okla.	Dean of Women
159. Pomona College	Claremont, Calif.	Dean of Women
160. Purdue University	Lafayette, Ind.	Dean of Women
161. Radcliffe College	Cambridge, Mass.	Dean
162. Randolph-Macon Woman's College	Lynchburg, Va.	Counsellor
163. Reed College	Portland, Ore.	Adviser
164. Rice Institute	Houston, Texas	Adviser
165. Ripon College	Ripon, Wis.	Dean of Women
166. Rockford College	Rockford, Ill.	Dean of Women
167. Rosary College	River Forest, Ill.	Dean of Women
168. Rutgers College	New Brunswick, N. J.	Dean of Women
169. Salem College	Winston-Salem, N. C.	Dean of Women
170. Seton Hill College	Greensburg, Pa.	Dean of Residence
171. Shorter College	Rome, Ga.	Dean of Women
172. Simpson College	Indianapolis, Iowa	Dean of Women
173. Shurtleff College	Alton, Ill.	Dean of Women
174. Smith College	Northampton, Mass.	Dean
175. Sophie Newcomb College of Tulane University	New Orleans, La.	Counsellor
176. South Dakota College of Mechanical Arts	Brookings, S. D.	Dean of Women
177. Southern Methodist University	Dallas, Texas	Dean of Women
178. Southwestern College	Winfield, Kan.	Dean of Women
179. Southwestern College	Memphis, Tenn.	Adviser
180. Southwestern University	Georgetown, Texas	Dean of Women
181. State College of Washington	Pullman, Wash.	Dean of Women
182. State University of Iowa	Iowa City, Iowa	Dean of Women
183. St. Laurence University	Canton, N. Y.	Dean of Women

Institution	Location	Title
184. St. Mary of the Woods College	St. Mary of the Woods, Ind.	Dean
185. St. Mary's College	Notre Dame, Ind.	Dean of Women
186. St. Olaf College	Northfield, Minn.	Dean of Women
187. Swarthmore College	Swarthmore, Pa.	Dean of Women
188. Syracuse University	Syracuse, N. Y.	Dean of Women
190. Tarkio College	Tarkio, Mo.	Dean of Women
191. Temple University	Philadelphia, Pa.	Dean
192. Texas Christian University	Fort Worth, Texas	Dean of Women
193. Thiel College	Greenville, Pa.	Dean of Women
194. Transylvania College	Lexington, Ky.	Dean of Women
195. Trinity College	Washington, D. C.	Dean of Women
196. Tufts College	Medford, Mass.	Dean of Women
197. University of Alabama	Tuscaloosa, Ala.	Dean of Women
198. University of Arizona	Tucson, Ariz.	Dean of Women
199. University of Arkansas	Fayetteville, Ark.	Dean of Women
200. University of Buffalo	Buffalo, N. Y.	Dean of Women
201. University of California	Berkeley, Calif.	Dean of Women
202. University of Chattanooga	Chattanooga, Tenn.	Dean of Women
203. University of Chicago	Chicago, Ill.	Chairman of Women's Council
204. University of Cincinnati	Cincinnati, Ohio	Dean of Women
205. University of Colorado	Boulder, Colo.	Dean of Women
206. University of Delaware	Newark, Del.	Dean
207. University of Denver	Denver, Colo.	Dean of Women
208. University of Detroit	Detroit, Mich.	Dean of Women
209. University of Dubuque	Dubuque, Iowa	Dean of Women
210. University of Georgia	Athens, Ga.	Dean of Women
211. University of Idaho	Moscow, Idaho	Dean of Women
212. University of Illinois	Urbana, Ill.	Dean of Women
213. University of Kansas	Lawrence, Kan.	Dean of Women
214. University of Kentucky	Lexington, Ky.	Dean of Women
215. University of Maryland	College Park, Md.	Dean of Women
216. University of Maine	Orono, Me.	Dean of Women
217. University of Michigan	Ann Arbor, Mich.	Dean of Women
218. University of Minnesota	Minneapolis, Minn.	Dean of Women
219. University of Mississippi	Oxford, Miss.	Dean of Women
220. University of Missouri	Columbia, Mo.	Dean of Women
221. University of Montana	Missoula, Mont.	Dean of Women
222. University of Nebraska	Lincoln, Neb.	Dean of Women
223. University of Nevada	Reno, Nev.	Dean of Women
224. University of New Hampshire	Durham, N. H.	Dean of Women
225. University of New Mexico	Albuquerque, N. M.	Supervisor of Women

INSTITUTION	LOCATION	TITLE
226. University of North Carolina	Chapel Hill, N. C.	Advisers
227. University of North Dakota	Grand Forks, N. D.	Dean of Women
228. University of Oklahoma	Norman, Okla.	Dean of Women
229. University of Oregon	Eugene, Ore.	Dean of Women
230. University of Pennsylvavnia	Philadelphia, Pa.	Directress of Women
231. University of Pittsburgh	Pittsburgh, Pa.	Dean of Women
232. University of Redlands	Redlands, Calif.	Dean of Women
233. University of Richmond	Richmond, Va.	Dean of Women
234. University of Rochester	Rochester, N. Y.	Dean of Women
235. University of South Carolina	Columbia, S. C.	Dean of Women
236. University of South Dakota	Vermillion, S. D.	Dean of Women
237. University of Southern California	Los Angeles, Calif.	Dean of Women
238. University of Tennessee	Knoxville, Tenn.	Dean of Women
239. University of Texas	Austin, Texas	Dean of Women
240. University of Toledo	Toledo, Ohio	Dean of Women
241. University of Utah	Salt Lake City, Utah	Dean of Women
242. University of Vermont	Burlington, Vt.	Dean of Women
243. University of Virginia	Charlottesville, Va.	Dean of Women
244. University of Washington	Seattle, Wash.	Dean of Women
245. University of West Virginia	Morgantown, W. Va.	Dean of Women
246. University of Wisconsin	Madison, Wis.	Dean of Women
247. University of Wyoming	Laramie, Wyo.	Dean of Women
248. Ursinus College	Collegeville, Pa.	Dean of Women
249. Vanderbilt University	Nashville, Tenn.	Dean of Women
250. Vassar College	Poughkeepsie, N. Y.	Dean
251. Virginia Institute	Blacksburg, Va.	Adviser
252. Washburn College	Topeka, Kan.	Dean of Women
253. Washington University	St. Louis, Mo.	Dean of Women
254. Webster College	Webster Groves, Mo.	Dean of Women
255. Wellesley College	Wellesley, Mass.	Dean
256. Wells College	Aurora, N. Y.	Dean
257. Wesleyan College	Macon, Ga.	Counsellor
258. Western College for Women	Oxford, Ohio	Dean of Women
259. Western Maryland College	Westminster, Md.	Dean of Women
260. Western Reserve University	Cleveland, Ohio	Dean
261. Westminster College	New Wilmington, Pa.	Dean of Women
262. Wheaton College	Norton, Mass.	Dean
263. Wheaton College	Wheaton, Ill.	Dean of Women

INSTITUTION	LOCATION	TITLE
264. Whitman College	Walla Walla, Wash.	Dean of Women
265. Willamette University	Salem, Ore.	Dean of Women
266. William Smith of Hobart	Geneva, N. Y.	Dean
267. Wilson College	Chambersburg, Pa.	Dean
268. Winthrop College	Rock Hill, S. C.	Dean of Women
269. Wittenburg College	Springfield, Ohio	Dean of Women
270. Yale University	New Haven, Conn.	Adviser
271. Yankton College	Yankton, S. D.	Dean of Women

C

QUESTIONNAIRES

I. QUESTIONNAIRE SENT TO THE PRESIDENT

TEACHERS COLLEGE
COLUMBIA UNIVERSITY
NEW YORK

December 2, 1926

My dear President:

In the effort to make the training of advisers of women more effective, we are asking you to coöperate with us by answering the three questions below and returning this sheet in the enclosed stamped envelope. We shall be very grateful for your help.

Harry D. Kitson
Professor of Education

Sarah M. Sturtevant
Associate Professor of Education

Name of Institution...

I. Does your institution have a woman *officially appointed* to supervise the various phases of college life among the women students: as academic programs, housing, social activities, vocational guidance?

Yes   No
....

II. Is her title Dean of Women....Adviser....Warden....Counsellor.... or some other?...

III. What is her name?...

....
President

144

II. QUESTIONNAIRE SENT TO THE REGISTRAR

TEACHERS COLLEGE
COLUMBIA UNIVERSITY
NEW YORK

May 8, 1926

To the Registrar:

Will you be so good as to give us the following information to be used for an intensive investigation of accredited colleges and universities? A stamped addressed envelope is enclosed for your convenience. We shall be exceedingly grateful for your help.

Very truly yours,

Harry D. Kitson
Professor of Education

Sarah M. Sturtevant
Associate Professor of Education

[Please do not detach]

. . . .

Name of Institution...

Location ....

Kindly indicate the number of students enrolled during the present semester *excluding those in extension and extra-mural courses:*

(*a*) men..................... (*b*) women.....................

III. VOCATIONAL HISTORY QUESTIONNAIRE
SENT TO WOMEN DEANS

Name of institution..

Location ....

(City)   (State)

145

I. Degrees

Kindly put a check (√) after the degrees you hold:

1. A.B.   2. A.M.   3. Ph.D.

If any other, please indicate ....

II. Teaching

a. Do you teach in addition to acting as dean of women?
b. If so, what subject?
c. How many hours a week?

1. The first semester? ....
2. The second semester? ....
3. In the summer? ....

d. If you teach, put a check (√) after your official *academic* rank:

1. Instructor   3. Associate professor
2. Assistant professor   4. Professor

If any other, please indicate ....

III. Experience

a. 1. How many years have you held your present position in the institution where you now are? ....
2. Please give your exact title. ....

b. How many years before taking your present position were you

1. Dean of women in a college?....Normal?....High School?....
2. Assistant dean of women in a college?........Normal?........ High School?........
3. Assistant to the dean of women in a college?.....Normal?..... High School?.....

c. In what occupations (include teaching) prior to becoming a dean of women did you earn your living for at least a year at a time?

....

IV. Salary

a. What is your present salary in cash

1. During the college year of ten months?......................
2. During the summer session? ....

b. Does the college give you living in addition?......................
c. Do you regularly serve as dean of women during the summer session? ....

(In no cases will individual figures be published. The aim is to find the extremes and the average.)

IV. QUESTIONNAIRE SENT TO WOMEN DEANS
FOR AN ANALYSIS OF THEIR DUTIES*

Name of institution ....

Location ....

Explanation: This information sheet has already been filled out by a number of deans of women. The average amount of time required is 25 minutes.

No specific data received will be published. The aim is to find the range and the averages.

Put an X after an item to indicate *yes.*

I. *Name of Dean:*

II. *Family:*

    a. Married
    b. Widow
    c. Divorced
    d. Dependents   Total .... Partial ....
    e. What relatives live with you?

III. *Church Connection:*

    a. Member?   *b.* Of what church?

IV. *Degrees:*

    a. A.B.   *b.* A.M.   *c.* Ph.D.   *d.* Any other?

V. *Professional Training:*

    Did you ever take a professional course preparing for the work of dean?

VI. *Academic Honors:*

    a. Phi Beta Kappa   *d.* Scholarships
    b. Sigma Xi   *e.* Honorary degrees
    c. Fellowships   *f.* Other honors

VII. *Travel:*

    Have you had foreign travel?

VIII. *Teaching:*

    a. Do you teach in addition to acting as dean of women?
    b. If so, what subject?
    c. How many hours a week?

* This questionnaire was sent to all women deans in colleges and universities approved by the Association of American Universities for the purpose of an analysis of their duties.

1. The first semester?....................................
2. The second semester? ....
3. In the summer? ....

    d. If you teach, put an *X* after your official academic rank:

1. Instructor
2. Assistant professor
3. Associate professor
4. Professor
5. If any other, please indicate ....

IX. Do you, in addition to acting as dean, perform any other important function, as that of

1. Librarian?
2. Registrar?
3. Head of placement?
4. Head of a department?
5. Some other?

X. *Experience:*

    a. 1. How many years have you held your present position in the institution where you now are?
       2. Please give your exact title.

    b. How many years before taking your present position were you
       1. Dean of women in

         a. College?   *b.* Normal?   *c.* High School?

       2. Assistant dean of women in a

         a. College   *b.* Normal   *c.* High School

       3. Assistant to the dean of women in a

         a. College?   *b.* Normal?   *c.* High School?

    c. In what occupations (if teaching, tell the type), prior to becoming a dean of women, did you earn your living for at least a year at a time?

                    Kind of Work   *Time*

    ....

    ....

XI. *Salary:*

    a. What is your present salary in cash

       1. During the college year excluding summer school?........
       2. During the summer session? ....

b. Do you usually serve during the summer session?
c. Does the college give you in addition
1. A house for yourself?
2. Room or rooms?
3. Board?
d. Do you live in a dormitory?
e. Do you perform dormitory duties?

XII. *Living Conditions of Women Students:*
a. Give the number for each of the following:
1. Number of dormitories managed by the college ....
2. Sorority houses ....
3. Coöperative houses ....
4. Off-campus boarding houses ....
5. Church dormitories ....

b. What other groups of women students who are organized as to living have you?

XIII. *Standing Faculty Committees:*
Please indicate by a check in the appropriate column whether your college has a STANDING FACULTY COMMITTEE dealing with each of the following in connection with women students or with both men and women students, and your relation to that committee. The names of the committees are not important.

COMMITTEE	(a) IS THERE ONE?	(b) ARE YOU A MEMBER?	(c) EX-OFFICIO MEMBER?	(d) CHAIRMAN	(e) UNOFFICIAL ADVISER
1. Academic Scholarship					
2. Admissions .					
3. Curriculum .					
4. Degrees					
5. Discipline ..					
6. Finance or Budget ...					
7. Health					
8. Housing of Students .					
9. Loans					
10. Scholarships					
11. Student Activities ...					
12. Others					

XIV. *Staff:* Please write in the number of these types of assistants that are directly responsible to you, and by a check in the appropriate column indicate whether you select each or approve the selection.

TYPE OF ASSISTANT	(a) NUMBER	(b) SELECTED BY DEAN	(c) SELECTION APPROVED BY DEAN
1. Assistant Dean of Women			
2. Assistant to the Dean of Women			
3. Heads of Halls (not Sorority Houses) ...			
4. Chaperons of Sorority Houses			
5. Social Director			
6. Paid Chaperons for Social Functions ...			
7. Vocational Director ..			
8. Dietitian			
9. Housekeeper			
10. Cafeteria Director			
11. Clerical Workers			
12. Secretary of Religious Organizations			
13. Any Others			

XV. *Public Speaking:* Estimate as best you can the average number of speeches per week including formal and informal, off-campus and on-campus, that you make during the college year, as, 1 a week, 5 a week.

XVI. *Interviews:* Estimate as best you can the average number of hours per week given by you and your office assistants to interviews

      a. with students   *c.* with landladies
      b. with faculty   *d.* with other persons

XVII. *Distribution of Duties:* The distribution of duties in colleges differs greatly. Some of those listed below are performed by practically all deans. Some are performed by only a very few. Please indicate in the appropriate column whether you in your institutions do *the following in connection with women students,* and if not, who does.

Social Duties	(a) Do You as Dean?	(b) Does One of Your Assistants?	(c) If Not, Who Does?
1. Work intimately with student government			
2. Advise with Panhellenic			
3. Supervise in general extra-curricular activities			
4. Supervise social calendar			
5. Approve chaperons for parties			
6. Personally chaperon parties ..			
7. Have charge of discipline in regard to non-academic matters			
8. Interview students in regard to their individual prob-lems, i.e., do personnel work			
9. Entertain many college visi-tors			
10. Entertain many college stu-dents			

Academic Duties	(a) Do You as Dean?	(b) Does One of Your Assistants?	(c) If Not, Who Does?
11. Determine admissions			
12. Have chief responsibility in regard to entrance ex-aminations			
13. Guide policy in regard to curriculum			
14. Supervise catalogue			
15. Make academic adjustments for students who fail in studies			
16. Have interviews with stu-dents on academic questions			
17. Administer student loans			
18. Administer scholarship funds			
19. Have responsibility for disci-pline on academic matters			
20. Give excuses for absence from classes for illness—for other reasons			

Duties in Connection with Health	(a) Do You as Dean?	(b) Does One of Your Assistants?	(c) If Not, Who Does?
21. Supervise food provided by the college			
22. Supervise housekeeping			
23. Supervise the infirmary			
24. Initiate health projects			
25. Give talks on health			
26. Secure speakers on health ...			
27. Inspect and approve off-campus lodging houses			

Duties in Connection with Vocational Guidance	(a) Do You as Dean?	(b) Does One of Your Assistants?	(c) If Not, Who Does?
28. Give vocational information .			
29. Secure persons who give it ...			
30. Systematically advise students in regard to vocations			
31. Have charge of part-time employment			
32. Have charge of permanent employment			

Administrative Duties	(a) Do You as Dean?	(b) Does One of Your Assistants?	(c) If Not, Who Does?
33. Select members of the college staff like the registrar, librarian, etc.			
34. Approve selection of college staff			
35. Selection of members of faculty			
36. Approve selection of members of faculty			
37. Conduct faculty meetings ...			
38. Approve plans for dormitories for women			
39. Approve plans for other college buildings			
40. Approve purchase of equipment for dormitories for women			
41. Approve purchase of equipment for other college buildings			
42. Meet regularly with the trustees of the college			
43. Interview the faculty on educational policies			
44. Raise money for the college ..			

Duties in Connection with Religion	(a) Do You as Dean?	(b) Does One of Your Assistants?	(c) If Not, Who Does?
45. Plan chapel exercises			
46. Regularly lead chapel exercises			
47. Regularly attend chapel			
48. Supervise the religious activities			
49. Secure speakers on religious subjects			

    a. Check (√) from the forty-nine duties listed above the three which take the greatest proportion of your time.

    b. Underline the two which take the greatest proportion of the time of your assistants.

XVIII. *Records:* Please indicate by a check in the appropriate column which of these records you have (*a*) for every woman student, (*b*) for special women students, and (*c*) which concerning every student are accessible to you in some other office.

RECORD	(a) FOR EVERY WOMAN STUDENT IN DEAN'S OFFICE	(b) SPECIAL CASES IN DEAN'S OFFICE	(c) IN OTHER OFFICES—ACCESSIBLE TO THE DEAN
1. Information about parents ...			
2. Secondary school record			
3. College residence			
4. Score on mental tests			
5. College academic grades			
6. College honors			
7. Scholarships			
8. Loans			
9. College health record			
10. Times disciplined			
11. College activities			
12. Vocational interest			
13. Employment during college ..			
14. Employment after college ...			

XIX. What other records do you keep in your office?

....

....

....

XX. Kindly list below other important duties you perform which have not been included in this information sheet.

(*a*)........................   (*d*)........................

(*b*)........................   (*e*)........................

(*c*)........................   (*f*)........................

D

TIME CHART FOR DEAN OF WOMEN
DAYS RECORDED: JUNE 1-15, 1926

HOURS	DAYS	CODE FOR KEEPING RECORD PART I—PROBLEMS	
8:00	1 2 3 4 5 6 7 8 9 10 11 12 13 14 15	Academic Questions	A-
8:15		Chaperonage	B-
8:30		Clubs (Students)	C-
8:45		Community Interests	D-
9:00		Discipline	E-
9:15		Dormitory Duties—Housekeeping	F-
9:30		Dormitory Duties—Social	G-
9:45		Entertainment of Visitors	H-
10:00		Excuses	I-
10:15		Housing Off-Campus	J-
10:30		Organization Off-Campus	K-
10:45		Personnel Work	L-
11:00		Public Speaking	M-
11:15		Reading in Dean's Field	N-
11:30		Religious Activities on Campus	O-
11:45		Social Calendar	P-
12:00		Social Functions	Q-
12:15		Sororities	R-
12:30		Student Government	S-
12:45		Vocational Guidance	T-
1:00			
1:15		Not Specified	U-
1:30			
1:45		PART II—ACTIVITIES	
2:00			
2:15		Attendance in Person	X
2:30		Correspondence	Y
—		Interviews with Dean's Staff	Id
—		Interviews with Other Faculty	If
—		Interviews with Landladies	Il
—		Interviews with Parents	Ip
—		Interviews with Students	Is
—		Interviews with Others	Io
12:00 Midnight		Planning Alone	Z